SILENCE INTO SERVICE

GERRY PIERSE CSsR

Silence into Service

A SIMPLE COMPANION TO CHRISTIAN MEDITATION

THE COLUMBA PRESS
DUBLIN 1992

This edition, 1992, published by
THE COLUMBA PRESS
93 The Rise, Mount Merrion, Blackrock, Co. Dublin, Ireland

Cover by Bill Bolger
Origination by The Columba Press
Printed in Ireland by
Colour Books Ltd., Dublin

ISBN: 1 85607 045 X

Contents

Preface

There is a picturesque little island forty minutes by motor boat from the main island of Cebu in the Republic of the Philippines. About thirty families live on its five hectares. It was a little paradise but for the fact that it had no source of water. The islanders had tried to dig often but gave up at about twenty feet deep. All their water had to be brought from Cebu. A five gallon can of water could cost one third of the normal daily earnings of a fisherman.

Then one day a water diviner was invited to the island. He marked a place and told them that they would get an adequate source of water at one hundred feet. Joy swept the island. Listlessness was replaced by new energy. They organised the simple mechanism for digging. They set up a tripod with a pulley at the apex, thirty feet from the ground. To this they attached a heavy metal bar with a sharp tip. Then, day after day, it was pull-drop, pull-drop, pull-drop. They set up some barrels of water beside the hole. A hose brought the water into the hole to soften the sand or soil or rock that was being penetrated and to wash out what had been dislodged. The islanders worked on, day after day, week after week, until they came to the source of life – water – from within their own island. Then they roasted a pig to celebrate.

What the water diviner was to that island, the discovery of the tradition of the Mantra has been to my life. Before discovering the tapes and writings of Dom John Main and Dom Laurence Freeman, I had been trying to pray in different ways but I was never fully satisfied. Like John Main, I too discovered that there was a rich Christian tradition for meditation reaching back to St Paul and the monks of the fourth century. The Mantra tradition rang true to me and gave me the determination to persevere. The Mantra, the constant repetition of the prayer word, became the pull-drop process, repeated again and again, in good times and in bad, through sand and clay or even solid rock.

Never in seven years have I felt the word bring me through to silence. I had no occasion on which to roast a pig! But I did notice

7

something else. That barrel seems to be always full, full of fresh
clear water. No matter how much it is used, it seems never to become empty. There is more energy for the Lord's work, a greater
capacity for unhassled availability, greater resilience when things
go wrong.

The embryo of this book is experience, the experience of twenty-
five years of priestly ministry, in a variety of roles, in the
Philippines before, during and after the era of Ferdinand Marcos.

They were years of working in parishes and on missions and re-
treats, where many people were 'saying prayers'. I wondered if
they were praying. For them, fulfilment of obligations seemed
more important than responding in love. They were years of involvement with formation, where one finds young people caught
in-between. They were caught between an old system, where all
values and principles come from above, and an evolving one
where they have to 'process' meaning out of their own experience. They were also caught in the discovery within themselves of
an angel and a devil, and did not find a prayer-form that led to integration and wholeness.

They were years of involvement in a Church that was burdened
with death and yet must bring forth life. It was a Church much
concerned with possessions, power and prestige as it fought to
preserve its institutions and bureaucratic ways. At the same time
it was a Church striving to be a Church of the poor. It was a
Church striving to be relevant in the midst of poverty and political repression. The time of political repression and violence came
to a head in the Marcos years. The violence of the right, 'the sal-
vagings', was met by the violence of the left, 'the liquidations'. It
touched me close to home when my classmate in ordination, Fr
Rudy Romano, was abducted in July 1985, and has not been seen
or heard of since then.

During those years, an evolution was taking place within the
Church. The Church saw its ministry as being in the service of the
whole person rather than just as a saver of souls. This led to its involvement in various socio-economic, and, later, developmental
projects. Pastoral agents became aware that the poor could never
be set free by development alone, but that they needed to work toward their own liberation. This period also took its toll. Many
died – pastoral agents trying to be the leaven, and simple people

who raised their voices in support. Of the pastoral agents involved, priests, religious and lay workers, some persevered but many gave up. Some turned to violence, others opted out and even joined the very institutions that they had been fighting. The most common experience was burn-out. Their energies became exhausted. Could this have been because there was not enough spirituality, or enough of the proper kind of spirituality, to maintain the individuals and the groups in their being with the poor?

I spent five years trying to pray the Christian Mantra, guided by the tapes and writings of John Main and Laurence Freeman, both Benedictines, and then, two more years leading parish meditation groups. Everyday, every meditation period during these years, I saw myself always as a beginner. I learned the need to begin again and again no matter how persistent the distractions were. I needed to become more humble. I had to overcome the obsession with success that is one of the biggest obstacles to prayer. Meditation is one of the few things that one can teach while being conscious of being a failure in it oneself.

This book was brought to birth by the challenge to give an eight day retreat to a group of ICM Sisters in Cebu in May of 1990. This challenge was literally an education, 'e-ducare', a leading out from within, for me. As I reflected on what I might share in leading others to meditate, I began to hear and appreciate the kingdom that was within me, the 'treasure buried in the field'.

Learning to meditate is like learning a language. It is a 'something from within', an intuitive skill, rather than a rational process. Children pick up a language without thinking. Adults, however, need a certain amount of rational explanation to start. It is the same with meditation. A certain amount of explanation may be necessary to prepare the way, but the most important thing is to get into experience. Start saying the Mantra.

In the early part of the book, *Silence,* I try to give some explanations about prayer in general and about the tradition of meditation in particular. Later the reflections become more inspirational. In the part called *Service,* we see that meditation energises us as pastoral agents working for the kingdom in today's world.

I think teaching meditation is particularly appropriate at present. The official model of Church in the Philippines is now the Basic Ecclesial Communities model. It is a model of Church where small groups come together and share their lives in the light of the Word of God. This suggests a big theological move from popular religiosity, where the emphasis is on a God 'out there', to a God 'who dwells amongst us', whose story is mixed up with our story. Meditation gives the next logical step – to be with God 'who dwells within us'. It complements and completes the cycle of the Basic Christian Community Church.

As a Redemptorist I feel great joy at sharing this preferred way of prayer. Our founder, St Alphonsus Maria de Ligouri was a Doctor of Prayer. He himself founded about three hundred prayer groups in the Naples of his time. He insisted that the Redemptorist would always teach 'mental prayer', even to the unlettered people in the mountains. Have we lost this confidence in the ability of ordinary people to pray, not just say prayers?

These reflections could be used by lay people, religious or priests, for a private or group retreat or just for a lead-in to meditation. Take one chapter, read it, reflect on it, leave it aside and meditate. When these talks were spoken, there were pauses when images came, one after the other. They could well be read in the same way.

Finally, I would like to thank the many people who have played a part in making these pages become a reality. First, the prayer groups who have helped me grow and clarify and simplify my understanding and application of the tradition. I am grateful to Merly A. Wenceslao, Letty L. Lim, Kaperiere Leef and Teddy Dominado for their generous help in correcting and typing the text. Finally, thanks to Fr Ramon Fruto, my Vice Provincial Superior who was always been very supportive.

John Main claims, in his book *Word into Silence,* that the Word of the Mantra brings one into silence. This silence disposes the heart for apostolate, it brings one into service. The Chinese have a saying: 'The best way to do is to be.' If I am to be a do-er of the word, I must first be with the word in silence.

We go from *Silence into Service.*

Gerry Pierse CSSR

How to Meditate

How to Meditate

According to John Main, to meditate is very simple – but this does not mean that it is easy:

'You just sit still and upright. Close your eyes lightly. Sit relaxed but alert. Silently, interiorly, begin to say a single word. We recommend the prayer-phrase 'Maranatha.' Recite it as four syllables of equal length. Listen to it as you say it gently but continuously. Do not think or imagine anything – spiritual or otherwise. If thoughts and images come, these are distractions at the time of meditation, so keep returning to simply saying the word. Meditate each morning and evening for between twenty and thirty minutes.'

Silence

Ways of Prayer

Prayer is engagement with reality – the supreme reality, God.

Let us look at how Mrs Lee engages with reality. Mrs Lee, now in her late sixties, was a practical nurse. For many years she had been a volunteer in charge of the old men's home in the rural town where she lived. Her services were greatly appreciated by the community, by the civic authorities who had a very limited budget, and especially by the old men for whom she was both mother and father. But times are changing. Mrs Lee is getting older and the Health Board is more conscious of professional qualifications. The Health Board is now getting national funding and may appoint a young nurse to 'help' Mrs Lee. At first she thinks the 'help' is great, but soon she finds out that the men may be old, but they are still men. When they need to have their pillows patted they call the young buxom one rather that the oldee. Now she begins to hear talk also about her being not qualified, and the 'injustice' of keeping a younger person out of a much needed job.

The world of Mrs Lee begins to fall apart. Within her she finds surges of resentment towards the old men who are so ungrateful, towards the Health Board which is so cruel, towards the young nurse who has dislodged her as sole ruler of her kingdom, and towards the community at large.

Mrs Lee is in each one of us. I have never known anyone at any depth who does not have some deep pain, a sense of having been misunderstood and treated unjustly, at some stage of life. What applies to Mrs Lee, applies to all of us.

Now Mrs Lee could be a person who does not pray. In that case, how she would deal with her present reality in terms of prayer is an academic question. She is just a do-gooder, an activist. She is a fire-truck that delivers what she carries but has no access to a hydrant. Non-praying do-gooders are not unknown even in the religious life.

Or maybe she 'says prayers'. She has her devotions, her rosary, and her Mass. She is most faithful to them and makes sure that her daily life does not distract her as she ploughs through them like a ship through the night. Her life and her prayers are, indeed, like two ships passing in the night. This kind of prayer has its value. It expresses faith in God. But it is very much faith in 'a God out there', a God who does not engage in our lives.

Or maybe she talks to God about her problems. She may tell him about how unfairly she had been treated, how heartless the Board has been, how ungrateful the old men are ... 'And, of course, Lord, if she had an accident ... Oh, no, no ... but then again ...' This is really a 'give me' type of prayer. God is there to give me what I want. This prayer is very selfish and it is doubtful if it deserves to be called prayer at all.

Out of this prayer, she may spiritualise her problem. 'Oh Jesus, I will offer this up with the cross that you carried.' She gives herself a spiritual tranquiliser that enables her to cope with life in a befuddled sort of way. When we live under anesthetic, even a spiritual one, we only half live. She may develop a robust martyr complex.

Or Mrs Lee could listen. She could listen to her feelings, she could listen to Scripture, she could hear God. She could listen to her feelings: 'I am feeling very hurt, why am I feeling this way? My God, how self-centred I am! All the while I thought I was doing this for you ... Thank you for this happening by which I realise that most of what I was doing was for myself. I see that it is my ego, my sense of self-importance that is hurt. Thank you, Lord, for sending someone who can help these people better than I can.'

Or she can meditate on the stories of Jesus. She can be with the disciples on the boat during the storm when Jesus was asleep ... he was asleep in her too ... But this storm has woken her up, has woken him up in her also. As she meditates the story and stories of Jesus, she sees how life comes from death, his death and her death. She can truly pray, 'Would that this chalice would pass from me; but not my will but thine be done.'

If Mrs Lee is listening in these ways, she will quickly find her feet, because her house is built on the rock of reality and she is being brought more in touch with it as she prays. She will recover her sweetness and the joy at the core of her being.

Or Mrs Lee may be a person who meditates. She may be a person who spends two or more periods daily saying her Mantra.

Through this, she has come to live at her own centre. This too is where the spirit of Jesus dwells, where God dwells. It is here, as St Paul tells us, that the Spirit is ever crying, 'Abba, Father'.

Living in this reality, she can chuckle at the false reality that her ego projects. She is very aware of all that is happening within and around her, but it leaves her unperturbed deep in her being.

This preferred way of prayer, meditation, is what this book is all about.

John Main and the
Tradition of Meditation

During the past forty years, many Christians have been seeking a deeper dimension, a more spiritual, a more interior dimension to their lives. Because of this, many have flocked from different parts of the world to listen to spiritual masters in India. Many have attended classes on Transcendental Meditation and on Zen. During this period, one man has stood out as a Christian teacher of meditation. That was John Main. To him goes the credit for re-discovering and re-teaching the rich Christian tradition of meditation and interiority, that has existed since apostolic times. He believed that the beginning of all renewal in the Church should be a contemplative renewal. According to Bede Griffiths, John Main is the best spiritual guide in the Church today.

For John, being rooted was very important. His roots were in the south of Ireland, though he grew up mostly in London, England. He was born in 1926 and baptised Douglas. Later as a Benedictine he took the religious name, John, by which name he is remembered now. He was the fourth of six children, in what seems to have been a very loving family. He had a broad education, but at seventeen, during the Second World War, he joined a special communications corps of the British Army. Later, he was to use many images about radio signals as he described meditation.

When the war was over, he tried the religious life for a while, but he soon left it to study law in Dublin, Ireland.

In 1954 he joined the British Colonial service in Malaya. One day he was sent to deliver a picture to an Indian monk, the Swami Satyananda. This holy man was to have a big influence on his life. They began to talk about spiritual things and the Swami undertook to teach John how to pray by saying the Mantra, or prayer word. 'The spirit of him who created the universe lives in our heart, and in silence is loving to all,' the Swami told him. He was given a Christian word as his Mantra.

In 1956 he returned to teach law at Trinity College in Dublin. If, during this period, he told any of his priest friends about his meditation, they treated it with suspicion or hostility. After the death of a nephew, he reflected more deeply on life and decided to join the monastery of the Benedictines in Ealing, England. As a novice he found it very hard to obey his novice master, who told him to give up meditation. He was learning to 'let go' of attachments, even spiritual attachments, and this was to become essential to his future teaching.

In 1970 he went to the United States where he was headmaster for five years of the Benedictine School in Washington. At this time he had a chance encounter with the writings of Augustine Baker, a seventeenth century English monk, which led him back to John Cassian, the fourth century teacher of St Benedict. There he discovered the same practice of meditation with the Mantra as he had learned from the Swami in Malaya. He was inspired by this to study further into the Christian tradition and found more and more proof of the tradition for meditation that went back to apostolic times. He resumed his life of meditation three times a day, and began to teach meditation to others. One of his disciples at this time was a young Englishman, Laurence Freeman.

He returned to Ealing and started a lay community of meditators. From then until his death in December 1982, his energies were directed into teaching meditation and forming communities of meditators. In 1976 he gave lectures in Gethsemane, the monastery of Tomas Merton. From there he moved to Montreal, Canada, where, with the support of Bishop Crowley, he started a monastery. Even though the priory no longer exists, the work of teaching Christian meditation continues. There are now meditation groups in twenty-five countries.

Fr John left behind him many books and tapes on meditation. Fr Laurence has also many tapes and has written two books, *Light Within* and *The Selfless Self*.

What were the main points of the tradition that John Main picked up and re-formulated for us today?

The first of these concerns ourselves. Each of us is disunited within ourselves. St Paul was aware of this disunity when he said, 'I cannot explain what is happening to me, because I do not do what I want, but on the contrary, the very things I hate.' (Rom 7:15) This lack of silence and interior harmony is all the more evident in today's world of radio, television, and consumerism. We are given little opportunity to live within ourselves or to be silent. We seldom live in the present moment. We are worried about the past, or planning for the future. We are distracted by our desires and illusions. St Augustine said, 'Man must first be restored to himself, that making in himself as it were a stepping-stone, he may rise thence and be borne up to God.' So a quiet period each day, in which we do not try to do anything but be aware of God's unfolding presence, is essential to restore us to ourselves. It is important for us to 'be still and know that I am God.' (Ps 46)

Our God is a God of love who so loved the world that he sent his only son, not to condemn the world, but to give it life. (Jn 3:16) Our God is a Father/Mother who loves us 'no matter what'. This is clearly shown in the parable of the prodigal son. Faced with this God we need to accept creatureliness. It is interesting that our first parents in the Garden of Eden were tempted by satan to 'become like God', to reject their creatureliness. The devil also tempted Jesus in the desert to work miracles and so reject humanness or creatureliness.

Creatureliness is accepting that God and not ourselves, our ego, is the centre of reality. We do this by the poverty of the single word, the prayer word, the Mantra. By continuing to say the Mantra we take the searchlight of consciousness off ourselves. As we remove ourselves from the centre of the stage, God finds his true place there.

God loved us especially in Christ, his beloved son. Each time we meditate we enter into the death and resurrection of Christ. He gave himself over to the will of his Father even unto death. In meditation we let go of all, we die. As we die to the self, the ego, we are reborn into Christ.

God's life is already ours. We are temples of his Holy Spirit. The Spirit of God is already praying in our hearts, crying, 'Abba, Father.' (Rom 8) Apart from this Spirit, we do not know how to pray. When we are present at our own centre, through the Mantra, we are into the flow of communication between the Father and the Spirit, we are in the prayer of Christ himself, pure prayer. We do not have to seek God's presence; he is already within us; we must just realise it. 'The kingdom of God is within you.'

The process of transformation is gradual, it needs perseverance. It takes time and discipline to unhook the ego. It means saying the

Mantra twice a day, everyday for the rest of our lives. It is a pilgrimage, a journey. The important thing is to begin; to begin soon and then to begin each time you sit down to meditate; to begin again each time you become distracted.

There is no argument to convince one of the validity of the claims of meditation. Talking about it only delays the process. Experience is the great convincer. When you have tried it for some time you will find a rightness about it that will make you know that it is really prayer. Possessiveness is our great weakness. This can even be spiritual possessiveness. When we pray with images and thoughts we are trying to grasp God who is beyond grasp. We may be giving ourselves nice feelings or satisfying thoughts. In meditation we grasp nothing, we want nothing. If something extraordinary happens in meditation, put it aside, it is a distraction. We apply the words of the Lord, 'Anyone who wishes to be a follower of mine must leave self behind, he must take up his cross and come with me.' (Mk 8:34) The tradition that has come down from apostolic times is that praying the Mantra is one of the best ways of carrying out this command.

Meditation and Silence

Some years ago the B.B.C. did a documentary film on St Bueno's Retreat Centre in North Wales. It showed the work of the centre, and people on retreat talking about their retreat experiences. The centre got the general feedback that people were very impressed, attracted to the idea, but that they would be terrified of the silence.

There is a growing lack of silence and fear of silence in today's world. There is so much noise and bustle and rushing that people do not know what to do with silence. Or maybe they are afraid of what silence would do with them! They are afraid of what would happen if they let what is inside themselves speak. Yet, if we are to know God, we must know ourselves first. St Augustine tells us and there is no way of being present to what is inside ourselves other than the way of silence.

To be silent we need silence of the body, silence of the mind and silence of the emotions.

Silence of the body
We are growing more conscious today of the connection between the physical and the psychological. If we are to be silent within, we need to be physically silent. When we begin to meditate we will often experience a restlessness, a wanting to get away from it. Sometimes we will almost feel our feet walking out the door or feel that the body has got up and left before realising that it has happened. There is a need, then, to tie down the body. It is good to have a definite time and place in which to be silent. We need this at least twice a day, in the morning and in the evening, for twenty to thirty minutes.

Silence of the mind
The next silence is silence of the mind. As we try to be still we find that we have several theatres within our heads, all showing their own internal movies. We can be reliving the past or enjoying fantasies about the future. One Indian writer said that the mind is like a tree inhabited by monkeys. They keep jumping from branch to branch and chattering at each other. It takes great patience with

ourselves to calm this turmoil and to stop the movies and the monkeys.

Silence of the emotions
The third kind of silence is an emotional one. As we try to be still, we may become aware of tension or unrest within. Very often this is due to anger or resentment which we may or may not be able to name. Psychological processing would say that these feelings should be brought out into the open and faced. This is often very helpful. Flight from them or repression are not helpful. By the silence of meditation we deal with these emotions in another way. We just stand our ground. We are not intimidated by them, we just sit still. Bit by bit this tenacity bears fruit in integration and calmness.

If there are three levels of silence needed to meditate, there are also three great obstacles to silence, namely, distraction, sleep and the *pax perniciosa*.

Distraction
Attention or attraction is to be pulled in a definite direction. Distraction is to be pulled in other directions. When we try to meditate, to be still, we find ourselves being distracted. Our desires, our regrets for the past, our plans for the future, all pull us in different directions. The ego is ever seeking to be lord of the manor. The Mantra tradition gives us a remedy for this. We focus on it, are drawn to it. When we get distracted we know exactly what to do to come into traction – just begin again to say the Mantra.

Sleep
Sleep is the second enemy of meditation. If you feel sleepy when you start meditating, the first reason may be that you are too tired. Then perhaps the best thing for you to do is to go and sleep first. In fact, one of the best times for meditation is after restful sleep. This is true especially at night. There is stillness, no telephone, no television, no children playing. This can be the answer for the people who say that they have no time to meditate. Meditate during the night. After some hours of sleep the body tends to wake naturally. Get out of bed and meditate. Then go back to sleep again. If you develop this rhythm you will find that your night has been more restful than if you had slept the whole night through without interruption.

But what if tiredness is not the reason for your sleepiness? Then it is very probable that it is avoidance. This is related to the third level of silence that I mentioned above. There may be something in your life – anger, resentment, an unforgiven hurt, a decision to be made – which you want to avoid. When you sit down to pray it will come up to challenge you. One way of avoiding it is to fall asleep. Here is where fidelity will give you the courage to stand your ground. Experts on dogs tell us that if you look a dog in the eye, no matter how fierce he is, he will not bite you. Saying the Mantra is like standing your ground and looking the anxiety straight in the eye. You are not fighting with it, or reasoning with it, or digging into its roots, but sooner or later as you continue to stand your ground in the face of it, whatever is disturbing you loses its power over you.

Pax Perniciosa

The last enemy, *pax perniciosa*, pernicious peace, is the most subtle. It is a state of mental vacuity or absorption during the time of prayer that could easily be mistaken for prayer. It could be a pious absorption or an absorption in one of our fantasies and it is discovered almost with regret. You have come to a *modus vivendi* with the distraction, almost come into friendship with it. The lazy part within you has enjoyed a break from the discipline of the Mantra. The tradition here is also very clear. As soon as this state is discovered, whether it is a state of genuine contemplative silence or mental vacuity or absorbing distraction, step firmly on it by saying the Mantra.

Silence is necessary to meditate, to realise the presence of Christ praying within us. This is a total silence of body and mind and emotions. Silence will be difficult to achieve because of distractions, sleep or pernicious peace. To achieve this silence, the little prayer word, the Mantra, is the means that the tradition gives us. The author of *The Cloud of Unknowing* tells us, 'Fasten this word in your heart so that it never leaves you, come what may. This word is to be your shield and your spear, whether in peace or in war. With this word you are to beat upon the cloud and the darkness above you. With it you are to smite down every manner of thought under the cloud of forgetting. So much so, that if any thought should press upon you to ask you what you would have, answer it with no other words but this little word.'

Meditation and other Traditions of Prayer

A good working definition of spirituality is 'the precise way in which this person, with his or her unique faith history, in this time and place, perceives and responds to God.' A very important part of this unique faith history will be the models of spirituality and prayer to which the person has been exposed.

In general there have been two models. The *kataphatic* tradition is one where words and images are used in prayer and it is generally associated with the West. It is also called the *via affirmativa* or affirmative way. The *apophatic*, or *via negativa*, is a way of prayer, of being present without images or words.

St Ignatius and the *Spiritual Exercises* would be a great example of kataphatic prayer. As one meditates through the gospel scenes and makes colloquies with Our Lord and Our Lady, one comes into deeper union with God. However, Ignatius moves very close to apophatic prayer when he speaks of the third method of prayer (par. 258 of the *Exercises)* which is 'a measured rhythmical recitation of the single word ...' This tradition also speaks of the Ignatian Day – which can be the day of one's life, of a thirty days retreat, a shorter retreat, or even of a period of prayer where there is movement from a more active morning to a more passive contemplative evening.

One of St Teresa's ways of explaining prayer, again in the kataphatic tradition, is in terms of the four ways of drawing water. At the beginning, prayer is like drawing water with a bucket – there is a lot of effort and little result. The next stage is using the windlass – today, we might say a hand pump – less effort gives more results. Then there is the irrigation system which, once it has been set up, delivers the water without too much effort on our part. Finally there is the rain, when God does everything and we do nothing. So, in Teresa, there is a progression from reasoning and thinking to a state where the senses are suspended and there is pure presence to God. There is a movement from the kataphatic to the apophatic.

St John of the Cross, though in the apophatic tradition, would basically insist on the same progression. For him, and those who follow him, one would have to have acquired certain habits of virtue before moving on to a higher stage of prayer.

This has generally been the model for progress in prayer in the Western Church for centuries. Teresa said that the water is for the flowers and the flowers are the virtues. As one moves from one stage to the other, there is a growing detachment from sin and growth in virtue. Any effort to accelerate this process is to be seen as pride. This model of prayer has produced great saints through the centuries and is to be much respected. Spiritual Directors in this tradition are justifiably very suspicious of techniques of meditation or anything that would give instant experiences. They would be even more apprehensive about commercialised meditation or 'solve your problem by meditation' (at a fee) groups.

However, there is an entirely different tradition in the Church, the tradition of Christian meditation as re-discovered by Fr John Main in his own experience and in the writings of John Cassian in the fourth century. This is the tradition of praying the prayer-word, the Mantra. By praying the Mantra one takes the focus of attention off oneself. One is following the call of Christ to leave self behind and follow him. It is a simple method, but not an easy one.

According to the Enneagram, each of us is either head-, heart- or gut-centred. According to where our priority area is, we will tend to indulge, during prayer, in fine ideas, soothing feelings or in the satisfaction of needs. Wallowing in any of these indulgences will tend to feed the ego. This will make our prayer counter-productive as it will not lead us away from ourselves and into oneness with God.

With the Mantra, on the other hand, there is no thought, no image, no feeling, no fulfilling of needs. There is just presence to the word which brings us to our centre where the Spirit of Christ dwells. This is a transforming presence.

A Zen saying goes like this:
'I looked at the mountains and the rivers.
They frightened me.
(Because of the rebels and wild animals lurking there).
I went into meditation. I saw nothing.
Afterwards, I looked at the mountains and the rivers.
They were just mountains and rivers.'

When one has being praying the Mantra for some time, friends will begin to comment on the change that they notice. 'There seems to be a new calm about you of late,' they will say.

To those trained in the kataphatic tradition, the claims made for the Mantra seem far-fetched and ridiculous. That is why John Main insists that these claims can only be verified by experience. Start saying the Mantra and you will know in a short time if it is right for you. Personal verification is essential. Nobody who has not made a serious effort to pray the Mantra for at least a few months, has the right to question the value and authenticity of this way of prayer.

I have a fear that the idea that holiness is the domain of specialists, monks and nuns, is partly due to the kataphatic tradition. Its insistence that it would be pride to seek to advance from one stage to another, without having first attained a certain level of virtue, sets a barrier to growth for the more timid who abandon the effort to 'professionals'. The division of growth into mansions or stages on a ladder may tend to play to our obsession with success even in spiritual things. It may indeed lead to pride at being 'worthy' to advance and hinder that very advance.

In praying the Mantra we are not concerned about success. We are concerned only about being faithful to a discipline, a discipline that detaches us from our self-centredness. This is a constant process that has no stages by which it can be measured. It is only what we notice in our daily lives that assures us that something has been happening.

Sometimes those of one tradition seem not to be able to see the point of view of the other, just as many Western trained doctors cannot accept the merits of acupuncture.

While it is more common to begin to pray with words and images, there is also a tradition and a proven practice of beginning with apophatic prayer. Anybody who makes the decision to start saying the Mantra will, of course, have made this decision out of some knowledge of the scriptures and the teachings of the Church, and a desire to live a more Christian life. Then as they continue to say the Mantra and experience the freedom and grace that it brings, they will be drawn to greater study of the scriptures and to a more simple, virtuous life.

Is the Mantra really Prayer?

The question is often asked, 'Is the Mantra really prayer?' My first answer is a story.

There was a village by a lake that had a beautiful Church and bell tower. However, during a geological movement of the earth, the whole village got buried in the water. Later, a tradition grew up in the place that the Church bells could sometimes be heard ringing.

A holy man was fascinated by this story and wanted to hear the bells. He spent a whole month on the shore, listening intently for the bells, but he never heard them. He decided to abandon his quest. As he could not hear the sound of the bells, he decided, on his last day, just to listen to the sound of the waves. It was then that he heard the sound of the bells!

When we seek the transcendent, we do not find it. When we listen to the immediate we hear the transcendent. I think this is what happens when we say the Mantra. We are present to the present moment in the here and now, and then we are also present to God, reality itself. But when we try to grasp this moment and this reality for itself we lose it.

This truth is borne out by many New Testament stories. At the transfiguration, Peter wanted to build tabernacles to retain the moment of transfiguration, to grasp the moment of the presence of God, but it was foolish talk. 'He hardly knew what he was saying.' (Mk 9:6)

The presence of the risen Lord, the Mystical Christ, is never known at the time of his presence. This is shown clearly in the story of the disciples on the road to Emmaus. Jesus joins the depressed disciples but they do not recognise him. He explains the Scriptures to them and again they do not recognise him. It is only in the breaking of the bread that they recognise him and then he is gone. It is only at this point, in retrospect, that they see that he has been with them all the time. 'Were not our hearts burning inside us as he talked to us on the road and explained the Scriptures to us?' (Lk 24:32) In praying the Mantra we are not aware of Christ, we are only present to the Mantra.

In retrospect we can see that being present to the Mantra we are present at our own centre and when we are present there we are where the Spirit of Christ is. Christ is in the Father. So we are present to God, in a sense, without knowing it. The only way we can be present to God is 'without knowing it.' We are praying 'without knowing it.' So it is true to say that when we know that we are praying we cease to pray, just as a saint ceases to be a saint when he knows that he is one.

Praying the Mantra, being present without knowing it, tells us also about how Christ is present when we serve others. There is a spirituality that says that we should love Christ in others, that we should see Christ in others. The problem about this is that we may be using others to get to Christ. So we do not love others for their own sakes but only because they bring us to Christ. We make them into 'things' that bring us to Christ. It seems to me to be much more true and wholesome to love others, period. When we love others we look at the human face, we see the brokenness, we respond to the person. And we find Christ. I think this is what St Augustine meant when he said, 'When one ministers to the sick it is Christ ministering to Christ.' Christ, in you, ministers to the sick, and Christ, in the sick person, ministers to you. This can be seen in retrospect but not at the time. Efforts to be 'religious', when what we are called to is to be human, can make our whole presence to others quite phoney.

The Mantra, then, is prayer because it makes us present to the transcendent while not grasping it. Praying the Mantra prepares us to minister to Christ, a Christ who is present in all human situations, but whose presence can best be seen in retrospect.

The Mantra – Crude but Efficient

When I was growing up in the south of Ireland, we used to fish by trolling a weighted spinner after our canvas currach. One day we were joined by an American bishop on an angling holiday. He came decked out with all the paraphernalia that consumerist genius could invent. He had fishing boots, fishing pants, a fishing jacket and a special fisherman's hat in which an assortment of flies were set. He had a variety of fishing rods. He had boxes of bait of different kinds, gut and line, weights and swivels. He looked disparagingly on our lines and spinners and said, 'You don't catch fish with those crude things do you?' Well, that whole afternoon he made his cast as the book told him to, but he caught nothing. Every time we landed a mackerel or a pollack, my uncle would hold it up and say, 'Crude but efficient, my Lord!'

When we talk about praying the Mantra I feel like saying the same. It is crude but efficient. It is an efficiency proved by tradition. The supermarket of prayer has many sophisticated theories and methods to offer but, to my mind, none is as simple or as efficient as the Mantra.

Navigation is another area that has become very sophisticated. But the ordinary fisherman has his own very simple and effective method. When he is going somewhere he takes a point on which he fixes the bow of his boat. The winds and the waves and the currents may ceaselessly try to knock him off course. But if he keeps coming back to that point he will make progress towards his destination. If he allows himself to drift with the current, or be sidetracked by the wind, he may end up going around in circles or going in the opposite direction.

The Mantra is the point on which the meditator sets his bow. He or she is attracted toward it and everything else is a distraction. It is the sure way, no matter how long it takes, to bring you to your destination.

Our generation has experienced great changes in the theory and practice of spirituality and formation. In the past there was a mould into which people were to be formed. Who God was and how he acted was clear. People responded to him by certain devotions and acts. All were required to fit into that mould. If you had any pains or hurts, you spiritualised them. You sealed them off by wrapping the sufferings of Jesus around them. This made the pain bearable, it anesthetised it, but the pain was still there. I am told that if a mouse goes into a beehive, the bees will sting it to death and then coat it with wax. This is what the process of spiritualisation does. But the putrid is still there and will stink with any change in temperature.

Today spirituality and formation are seen from a personal perspective. When God gives himself he gives us a self. In discovering this self we open the door to discovering him. This will mean facing up to the fixations and hurts that come from the past. There is much counselling and therapy in modern formation, to unblock the blockages to flowing freely to the Lord. Undoubtedly a lot of this is good and profitable, but I think there is a limit to it.

If you have a pond that is overgrown it is good to rake out the weeds and the rubbish, but a point comes where the raking must stop and the water be allowed to settle if you are to see its purity and beauty. If there is a wound that has not healed because of hidden dirt within, it may be necessary to open the wound and wash it out, but a time quickly comes when tinkering with it is counterproductive. We have to stop picking at it and let it heal by itself.

So too with our selves. A certain amount of processing may be of value, but healing takes place in silence and cannot be pressured. It is when we stop picking at the self, when we take our attention off the self, that healing takes place. This is what happens when we pray the Mantra. We stop picking at ourselves and allow healing to take place. It is an unsophisticated method, simple but effective.

There are some who think that meditation is another form of introversion, of focusing on one's self, but it is the very opposite. It is focusing away from self. There are some who think that meditation is a form of passivity, but again this is untrue. Being before the Lord in silence, one experiences integration and a healing activity that is often far more effective than a lot of our sophisticated therapy. The healing that happens releases abundant energies for service.

What is a Good Meditation?

Recently I had a visit from a parishioner who was very upset about communion in the hand. She kept on repeating, 'How can God be placed on the ordinary, on dirty hands?' Religiosity leads people to seek God in the extraordinary, in visions, miracles, locutions, in special experiences. Christianity teaches us to experience God in the ordinary. Christ was constantly rejecting the demand for signs and wonders. This desire for the extraordinary can be a great obstacle to spiritual progress, because it can prevent us from recognising Christ where he is usually found, in the ordinary.

Jesus tells us in the Beatitude, 'Blessed are the pure of heart, they shall see God.' (Mt 5:8) What does pure of heart mean? Does it mean somebody who has never experienced temptation, someone who lives in an antiseptic, isolated, trouble free world? I do not think so. The Spanish writer Unamuno put it this way:

> Those who believe they believe in God
> But without passion in their heart,
> Without anguish of mind,
> Without uncertainty,
> Without doubt,
> Even at times without despair ...
> Believe only in the idea of God,
> Not in God himself.

Purity of heart and the recognition of God are rooted in daily reality. They are not found in ecstasy but in struggle. The pure of heart are seldom aware that they are pure of heart. They are just trying to be faithful and the words, 'Lord, have mercy on me, a sinner,' are much more likely to be on their lips than the words, 'Thank you, God, that I am not as the rest of people.' Sanity has been defined as having the same sickness as everyone else. Insanity, living outside of reality, is thinking that we are unique! To have a pure heart, then, is to be struggling to be faithful in a jungle of impurity.

To ask who is pure in heart is, in a sense, to ask a wrong question.

Purity of heart is a direction rather than an achievement. To ask what is a good meditation is to ask the same kind of wrong question. To meditate is to be going in a direction and to be casting off all baggage that will delay one or distract one on the journey. Meditation is not to be luxuriating in a successful achievement and stroking the ego, but to be struggling along a rocky road on which there are all sorts of obstacles and distractions. Meditation is faithfulness in going in the same direction, not the achievement of the end. If God gives moments of special joy or awareness of himself, they are to be accepted gracefully, but, when these moments are sought for themselves, they become an obstacle to meditation.

There was a man who died and was told that he would have to walk a million miles before he could enter heaven. He said that this was impossible and so he lay down where he was. After a million years, he realised that if he had walked even one mile a year he would now be in heaven. So he began to walk. As he began to walk, he found himself carried along by a joy that made the miles seem shorter and made him discount any difficulties experienced on the way.

What we need is to set out on the road of meditation each day, with courage and fidelity, and not to be self-consciously asking ourselves whether or not our meditation is a good one.

The Mandala Journey of Meditation

On the cover of this book there is a Mandala, a figure made up of concentric circles of blue, red and white. It is used in meditation in many Eastern traditions. It is used to help concentration, to help one focus as one begins to meditate. There are many such techniques in Zen and they are of value to those who follow that way.

Christian meditation, however, recommends the discipline of the Mantra and that only. Other ways may be useful, but if we chop and change, we may not persevere in any of them or we may fail in achieving depth.

Prayer may be compared to courtship. A boy or girl may court anyone they wish, but the time will come when they must choose a special person. That relationship must grow by concentrating on it. So too with meditation. We must concentrate on it once we have decided to go into it.

Again, prayer may be compared to digging a well. If we give up after ten or twenty feet and start again somewhere else, we will never get to any depth.

Praying the Mantra is like lighting a fire with a magnifying glass. We must focus on one method and one Mantra. Playing around with different Mantras or different ways of prayer prevents conflagration.

However, the Mandala can be a fascinating aid to help us understand what happens when we pray the Mantra. It does this on three levels:

What is happening in our meditation?
What is happening to ourselves in our daily lives?
What is happening in the meditation group itself?

First, let us consider the colours. On the outside there is blue (in fact this is the predominant colour), then there is white and then jagged turbulent red. The red fades into blue and then there is some nice white again. This reoccurrence goes on all the way to the centre. Around the centre there is a very jagged piece of red and then the central circle has blue with a pinprick of white.

The colours are symbolic. The blue is ordinary life. It basically symbolises smooth sailing accompanied by pleasant daydreams and distractions. In the blue everything is manageable. Meditation is pretty easy. 'Why all the fuss about it?'

Red is the time of turbulence, when there is nothing but distraction, when everything seems to be going wrong.

Then there is white. This is when there is great joy and even euphoria.

Moses was a good man, living in the blue. Then he had his experience of God in the Burning Bush, a great joyful white moment. But when he had to lead the people, he was into red often, in conflict with the Pharaoh and encountering hostility even from his own people.

Meditation gets more difficult as we go along. After a happy blue period, we may find ourselves getting angry and ill at ease for all sorts of reasons. We want to run away from it. Why invest in something that is getting us nowhere? But if we persevere, the blue returns and it may even give way to white.

This happens in the process of meditation. There are times when it is easy, times when it is sweet, and times when it is deadly difficult.

So too with the life of a meditator. One's life may go on in a routine way, then one experiences high moments of fervour and joy, which give way to times of turmoil and distress.

The prayer group too may begin with a certain joyousness, but an uncertainty about one another in the group can develop. After a retreat or a good sharing, the members may experience a great feeling of closeness. But then irritation, jealousy, anger, appear and the group seems ready to rip apart again. Then the cycle begins all over.

Whether we are talking of the journey of meditation itself, or that of our personal life, or the journey of the meditation group, there is only one thing necessary: to keep on saying the Mantra. The journey always leads inward. Some may drop off along the way, but faith will be growing among those who persevere.

The three colours may also be seen as expressive of the Trinity. The Father is in his blue heaven. The Son has his turbulent passage through this earth bringing him, through the Spirit, to resurrection. With each progressive cycle there will be more confidence in the presence of the Spirit deep within us and we will be less rattled by the transient and the external.

In the Mandala. the circles get smaller as they go inward. As we go inward we may not be conscious of coming nearer to the centre but we really are moving closer to it. The important thing is the direction in which we are travelling. It is the Mantra that assures us of that direction.

Always a Beginner

From time to time, we appeal for volunteer catechists in the parish. A whole range of people apply, from those who have just finished school to retired principals with PhDs in Education. By and large, the former are more satisfactory than the latter. The students are receptive, full of wonder, willing to learn, empty and ready to be filled. The PhDs do not see the point of the briefings. They think that they already know everything since they've been teaching all their lives. They abhor the simplicity of the procedure and of the presentation.

When we come to prayer, we have the same difficulty. If we feel that we are good at it, or know all about it, we are in great danger. If we feel empty, that we are beginners, there is a good prognosis for us. It was only when Peter said, 'Depart from me for I am a sinful man,' that Jesus called him. (Lk 5:8)

The call to follow Christ is a call to discipleship, to being a beginner, to accepting simplicity, to bowing to a discipline. Any notions that we may have about ourselves spiritually are great blocks to true spirituality. St Paul tells the Corinthians, 'When I am weak then I am strong.' (2 Cor 12:10) A sense of our own poverty, of our own weakness and sinfulness, is an essential prerequisite for true prayer.

God is calling each of us to fullness of life, to a great expansiveness of our potential. The first and main obstacle to our response is our own conceit, our ego's unwillingness to admit that we need a simple path to discover the fullness of life that is within us.

For St Teresa, the sense of our own sinfulness was the bread that was the staple diet accompanying all levels of prayer. For St Ignatius, freedom, and indifference to praise or blame, success or failure, was the goal of all spirituality.

The ego is the big block to true prayer and to true spiritual freedom.

Throughout the centuries much of the richness of our original Christian heritage has been lost. After the Arian heresy in the fourth century, which claimed that Christ was less than the Father, the Council of Nicea declared that he was one with the Father. This led to an over-swing in Western spirituality to seeing God as a mighty Father out there – a transcendent God to whom we ran for favours. The fact that this God became human in Christ and dwelt amongst us, was very much neglected. Even more neglected was the fact that our God continues to be with us, to be indwelling in us, through his Spirit. True prayer is getting into the stream of prayer that is happening in our hearts, where the Spirit of Christ is ever crying, 'Abba, Father.'

Presence in silence to this prayer within us is true prayer, and true prayer is transforming. You cannot be silent with the Spirit and continue to be destructively angry, fearful, jealous, revengeful, lustful. Either prayer will stop or these feelings will undergo purification. There is a wonderful line in *The Power and the Glory* by Graham Greene. Of the whiskey priest he says, 'He wanted to pray, but he knew that to pray is to act and he was not ready to act.' True prayer leads to the elimination of what is inconsistent with it. St Augustine put this in another way when he said, 'Love God and do what you will.'

To pray, then, we need to leave self behind. Each time we come to prayer we are beginners. We need to be humble. We need to be child-like in accepting a discipline that is simple and effective. There are many paths of prayer but I have come to be convinced, through my own experience and the experience of others that I have journeyed with, that praying the Mantra has a pre-eminence that cannot be denied.

Golf is a simple game that can be played by amateurs or professionals. It is a simple game yet one in which one can always improve. There is no score that cannot be beaten. Every stroke is a new beginning. The amateur can get a hole-in-one, the professional can miss a six-inch putt. So too with meditation. It is a prayer form for all. Every moment needs attention. One may become more proficient in it but one can never rest on one's laurels. Every stroke needs attention as if it were the first time one had even held a club. Every meditation period and every moment of meditation is a new beginning.

Meditation is a way of prayer for all. There is no one so uneducated that he or she cannot meditate. There is no one so far advanced that the discipline of meditation will not help him or her on the way. Just remember the heights of spiritual growth to which St Paul challenged his listeners. And who were his listeners? They were the ordinary folk of his time.

What we need is the courage to begin to meditate. When we have begun, we will experience a rightness about it and then we will not need to be convinced anymore. We will discover that the Mantra has the merit of displacing the ego, of unhooking our illusions.

It is simple beyond words, but that does not mean that it is easy. Our failure to do something so simple will bring us to a great humility, a great sense of poverty. It demands great courage and humility to begin to pray it, to begin each day, to begin again each time we become distracted, to be always a beginner. But 'taste and see' and you will find that 'the Lord is good.' (Ps 34:8)

Become as Little Children

People were bringing their children to him to have him touch them, but the disciples were scolding them for this. Jesus became indignant when he noticed it and said to them, 'Let the little children come to me and do not hinder them. It is to just such as these that the kingdom of God belongs. I assure you that whoever does not accept the reign of God like a little child shall not take part in it.' Then he embraced them and blessed them, placing his hands on them.' (Mk 10:13-16)

The supreme lie in all of our lives is to think or feel that we are the centre of the world. As long as we live out of that assumption we will exert every effort to defend it. We will build a wall of protection around ourselves and fight off any one who threatens us. So we accumulate goods, prestige and power. We get sucked more and more into protecting our position. The ego is at the centre of life. In traditional theological terms, this is called Original Sin.

The supreme truth, on the other hand, is that God is the centre of the world. When we learn this, we let go of the compulsive grasping for the false gods in which we tend to find refuge. When we let go of these, we find not loss but freedom. We find that our lives become more simple, more transparent, freed from anxiety.

I think this is what Jesus meant when he said, 'Unless you become as little children you shall not enter the kingdom of heaven.'

Children have no problem accepting dependence. They know that Mom and Dad are big and strong and that's just the way it is, that's okay. It does not mean that they are unaware of their own power to influence and irritate Mom and Dad, but they do recognise and accept that their parents are the source of all power for them. So, too, we need to recognise and accept that we are children of God and that all that we have is his gratuitous gift to us.

Children trust and are trusting. They are transparent before we adults teach them intrigue. They believe what is told to them and say what they believe. I was on a bus recently and I heard a mother say to her child, 'Stay there on your seat because there is a snake under it.' Yes, the child did behave well then, but would soon learn not to trust what the mother or others said.

Children do not think, do not analyse. They accept the world presented to them in its totality and in complete faith. They have no knowledge other than that which is presented to them. If they are told about a world of snakes or fairies, they believe it totally.

Children have great powers of concentration. When they are watching something that catches their attention or playing a game, they do it with great single-mindedness.

If we are to enter the kingdom we must change and become as little children. I believe that one of the best ways to change is to start saying the Mantra. When we say the Mantra we take the focus of attention off ourselves. We are no longer concerned with the false gods that we have to build around our ego as we try to defend it. As we take the focus off ourselves we come to sit calmly at our own centres. That is where Christ is, too. We find ourselves comfortable there with him. We can look out at the world through his eyes. It is a strange thing that we can easily, joyfully, cohabit in our own centres with Christ, but he can never move in with us. If we persist in keeping our false selves, or egos, dominating our centres, we keep his presence submerged and unrecognised.

The child lives in a transparent world. Through saying the Mantra we will also learn transparency.

The Zen Master had a disciple called Banki. Banki was blind but, because he was blind, he could see many things that others could not see. When his Master died, Banki said,

> When other people express grief, I often hear joy.
> When others express joy, I often hear jealousy.
> But when my master expressed joy, it was joy
> and when he expressed grief, it was grief.

Through praying the Mantra, we too come to a more genuine child-like alignment of our feelings and responses.

Children do not think. They accept holistically in faith. When we are saying the Mantra, we are not thinking of anything, not even of God. We are not grasping. We are just being with the totality – the God who dwells within us. It is only when we become as little children that we can do this. And the way to it is the way of the Mantra.

Meditation and the Word

In our meditation groups, we begin each meeting with reflection on Scripture, usually the gospel reading of the previous Sunday. I have found that every reading of the word of Scripture led me to speak about the word that is Christ and the word that is the Mantra. When we read the word of Scripture it opens to us the word of Christ and we discover how the word of the Mantra leads us to live more deeply in his presence. The three words form a triangle and you can start moving in any direction within it. The word of the Son of God moves one to the Scriptures which lead one to being in his presence with the Mantra. The Mantra leads us to his presence or to his word in Scripture. Any one of the three leads to the other two.

What is distinctive about Christianity? What is distinctive is that it is a religion based on a God who engages himself in the history of the world. This God is revealed progressively through story – stories in the book that we know as the Bible, and the stories of our own lives that are situated in the world where we encounter him today.

Our historical God reveals himself to us in story, his-story. His story, the Bible, is a library of books using all sorts of different styles – poetry, parable, history. In these various ways, God was telling us about himself in the only way in which we could hope to grasp anything about him. He was using our human nature. When something gets too big for us, we instinctively go into symbol or metaphor. When boy-meets-girl and is swept off his feet with infatuation, he may turn to poetry or metaphor to express his feelings. The beauty of the rising sun, the birth of a child, the beauty of a flower, all of these force us to say, 'I can't really describe it … it was like …' And so all sorts of literary devices were used by God to give us some glimpses of himself. We are told of how he created all things and made them good, reflections of his own goodness. Then he created humans 'in his own image, male and female he created them.' Each progressive story tells us about God - Noah, Abraham, the Exodus, David – all fantastically rooted in humanity, with its foibles and weakness.

Last but not least, he sent his own son who became Emmanuel,

God-with-us, who pitched his tent in our midst. Jesus, through his stories, further unveiled the Almighty. On leaving this world he sent us the Holy Spirit to be with us always, indwelling within us, and ever in a stream of love and prayer with the Father. This God and this Spirit and this story continue in our world and in our stories up to the present time. Pure prayer is within us. St Paul tells us that we do not know how to pray apart from this prayer.

In the *Constitution on the Liturgy* of Vatican II there is a very simple but deeply significant line (*Sacrosanctom Concilium* No. 37). It says that the celebration of the Sacraments should always be accompanied by an appropriate reading from Scripture. The energy of the Lord is in the story. The word of Scripture releases the word of God. As this idea is 'too big for me,' I will try to explain it by a story.

Once upon a time there was a Rabbi who used to dance when he prayed. When he prayed a solemn prayer it was a solemn dance and when he prayed a joyful prayer it was a joyful dance. The Rabbi died. Many years later there was another Rabbi who loved to tell the story about the Dancing Rabbi. But this second Rabbi had a problem – he was paralysed from the waist down. One night, as he was telling the story of the dancing Rabbi, he was so engrossed in the story, and the audience were clinging to his words so intently, that suddenly he got up and danced!

The power was in the story. The power is still in the story.

The story of Christ still has this power. This can be seen clearly in the *Spiritual Exercises* of St Ignatius. In the thirty days of the *Exercises*, the retreatant is led into contemplation of the life of Christ. He or she is invited to live in the stories and to let these stories mingle with the retreatant's own story. As this mingling takes place, and as the happenings are shared with the retreat director daily, the retreatant experiences that God is personal to him or her. There is a movement from a God 'out there' to a God who is interested in me. Then there is a further movement from the God who is interested in me to the God who dwells within me. There is a movement from the historical Christ of the synoptic gospels to the mystical Christ of St John and St Paul. There is movement from prayer to the transcendent God in heaven (worship), to the incarnate God on earth (reflection on God's presence on earth), to the indwelling Spirit within us (meditation).

The method of St Ignatius is one that has proved its value. It brings one through the Scriptures to intimacy with Jesus. It uses words and images to do this. But words and images are mercenaries. We use them to do a job for us. They are by nature limited and can even be subversive. They are incapable of expressing the whole reality of God. They can only give little pointers in the direction of God. God can never be grasped by words or images. Words and images can create the hunger that leads to silence, to pure being with God, to *con-templare*, to living in the same house with God. Then in meditation we be with God without words or images.

However, reflection on Scripture is not the only starting point. With considerable support from tradition and validation from experience, we can start to meditate in silence. We can start to put aside all words and thoughts and images and just be in his presence. The tradition has shown that saying the Mantra – the poverty of the one little word – is the best way to be released from the limitation of words and images themselves. Through the Mantra we learn poverty before God. And it is only when we are poor and empty that he can fill us, that he can dwell in us.

When we become one with God in meditation we find ourselves hungry at other times to know more about him and so we go to the Scriptures. The Scriptures then speak to us in a new way because of the faith and the openness that was born in us through meditation. Simplicity leads to richness and richness brings us back again to simplicity.

So we are back to the word, the holy trinity for meditators: the word Christ, the word in Scripture, and the prayer word, the Mantra. Each includes the other as each person of the Blessed Trinity encompasses the others.

Meditation and the Trinity

There is a story about myself when I was a small child. I had a pet rabbit. One day our dogs killed the rabbit. The older members of the family wanted to take the rabbit to bury it but I would not let it go. 'Wait till Daddy comes home,' I cried, 'Daddy will fix it.' That was the stage in my life when my parents, those who gave me life, were essential to sustain my life and were seen as all-mighty.

Later I went to the seminary and was ordained a priest. When I visited my parents as a young priest, it was a very different experience. I was a professional man in my own right, we enjoyed each other's company and argued with each other as adults on an equal footing.

In recent years it has been a different experience again. My parents were aging and they needed a lot of help. But the greatest joy was being with them – often there were long silences, punctuated by reminiscences or anecdotes – then back to watching television, reading the newspaper or a book again. There was a joy in just being together.

Now, the parents I lived with at these three stages were the same individuals. Yet in terms of relationship they were different persons altogether. There was a period of total dependence on them, a period of interaction with them, and a period of being with them when they depended more on me for action.

This is as near as I can get to understanding the Blessed Trinity. God Father/Mother is in heaven; we were made by this God, who is faithful and loving even when we are naughty. Then this same God, but as a different person, came and dwelt amongst us. He shared our joys and sorrows. He died and rose again and he now dwells on amongst us in his Spirit. This Spirit is in the Church of which we are members. Each of us is his temple in the same way as the Church itself is his temple. Each of us is a member of his sacred body, his arms and legs, lips and ears. He now depends on us to show his presence on earth.

The Church in recent centuries has lost touch with the Trinity.

With the Latin liturgy and a proliferation of devotions, God was mainly a God 'out there', a transcendent God, a Father God in heaven whom we could not touch. The Church itself was seen as a refuge, a place to run to in trouble, and where one asked for more or less miraculous solutions for one's problems.

Today, the preferred model of Church is that of the people of God. In many places, this way of being Church is expressed in building Basic Christian or Ecclesial Communities. In these communities, Christ is present through his Spirit. The Spirit of Christ is found in the community that is formed around the word of God, shares its concerns, and makes concerted action to solve its own problems. God is experienced as an incarnate God, a companioning God sharing with the people in their struggles. These communities soon realise that God is present amidst them as Spirit. This God demands our counterpart to his gifts. We are the members of his body, we are his hands and his feet. We are now in the theological period when he depends more on us to make his presence known in the world.

The growth of meditation groups is a continuum of the process of a new awareness of the totality of God. They can arise from or lead to Basic Ecclesial Communities. The kingdom of God is the place where God dwells. The transcendent Father is in heaven, but the Son became incarnate amongst us and his kingdom is here within our struggling communities. His kingdom is also within each of us. In meditation we realise this indwelling presence and become energised with the fullness of his life so as to become his hands and feet and lips in today's world.

Meditation and Moments of Christ

When they had finished making a fool of him, they stripped him of his cloak, dressed him in his own clothes, and led him off to crucifixion.

On the way out they met a Cyrenian named Simon. This man they pressed into service to carry the cross. Upon arriving at the site called Golgotha (a name which means Skull Place) they gave him a drink of wine flavoured with gall, which he tasted but refused to drink.
(Mt 27:31-34)

I remember a doctor telling me that a good part of his time was spent in reassuring people that there was nothing wrong with them. Then sometimes he would wake up at night remembering some patient and frightened that he had missed something serious. There are precious moments in all of our lives, moments when conversation or relationship could go deeper, and if they are missed they are lost forever. In fact, as we look at our lives we see that the great moments are the ones that just happened by themselves, or maybe were even forced upon us. We may have been able to notice them to our advantage or lose them forever. Most of our great plans and projects, on the other hand, really never come to anything.

The Gospels are full of such moments. One of the greatest, to my mind, was that of Simon of Cyrene who was forced to carry the cross of Jesus. It was just an ordinary day for him. He was going into town. He was not a 'religious' man. He met a crucifixion procession and did not want to have anything to do with it. He was dragged in unwillingly. But he took up the cross and carried it. He was one of the few people who helped Christ that day and will be remembered forever because of it.

This scene with Simon is a paradigm of the passion itself. Christ did not want to carry the cross either: 'Father, would that this chalice would pass from me, but not my will but thine be done.' Yet he accepted the cross that was given him. It was not a way of salvation that he had fashioned for himself. Yet, it was this uncontrived act that brought about our salvation.

We too are often absorbed in our plans, even plans for God's king-dom. We get so annoyed with the interruptions and unscheduled happenings. We waste so much energy in grumbling about the opportunity and lack of consideration of others. Yet, God's king-dom is in these moments.

On the road to Calvary, Jesus took time out to console the women and he gave assurance to the good thief on the cross. Even at these times of terrible personal stress he was able to take the focus of at-tention off himself and be concerned for others.

He turned the chance meeting with the woman at the well side – when he was just making a short-cut through Samaria – into an encounter of grace. He rewarded with a miracle of healing the tenacious faith of the men who let the cripple down through the roof during his grand sermon.

In the Old Testament also we find many figures who had great-ness thrust upon them. Jonas, Job and Jeremiah were all people who did not want to be where the Lord placed them, but respond-ed willingly enough to the inconvenient call.

We seem to be always selecting where to find God, rather than recognising him where he turns up. There is a story about a man who went to the Guru and asked how he would become holy. The Guru told him to practice seeing God in all things. He went on his way through a narrow forest path and met an elephant. The little boy riding the elephant shouted to him to get out of the way. But he reasoned like this: 'God is in the elephant. God is in me. God cannot hurt God. So I will just continue.' And so he did, in spite of the warnings of the little boy. When the elephant got close, he took the man up in his trunk and flung him into the forest out of the way. The man went back to the Guru full of complaints. He said that he had tried to follow the Guru's instructions and this was the result. 'But you did not follow my instructions,' said the Guru, 'God was also in the little boy.'

We miss the presence of God so easily. We get so impatient with interruptions: that troublesome phone-call; that beggar who turns up at the worst time. The companion who wants to pour out his or her problem when we have just about as much as we can carry ourselves. That companion who needles us and yet needs us to just *be* for him or her right now. We will miss these moments again and again if we cannot just *be*. These may not be 'religious' moments – they may be moments that make us feel like cursing, but these are the moments of Christ. These are moments when we are called to take the focus off ourselves and to be totally for others.

We often talk about when things get back to normal. But that time ever comes; the abnormal is normal, it is the time of Christ. Now is the time of salvation.

Can we train ourselves to be present to the present moment, the moment of Christ? I know of no better way than the discipline of the twice daily saying of the Mantra.

Faithfulness, not Success

One time I was planning to explore a cave with a friend. I asked him how far in we would go. He answered, 'Just far enough that we can say that we were there.'

I think his answer is indicative of a great problem of our times and particularly a great problem about meditation.

Life today offers so many opportunities and challenges that it is hard for young people to make a commitment to any one of them. This is true in marriage, religious life and in work. People want to keep their options open and not to give their all to any one thing. It is a far cry from the man in the gospel who, on finding a pearl of great price in a field, went and sold all that he had and bought the field.

This hesitation about making a commitment takes a severe toll on our lives. When we do not make a commitment we are free, but free too to be alienated, to be without roots or a 'something' or a 'someone' to anchor our hearts. This is the root of shallowness and boredom. John Main calls it *acedia*.

St Ignatius warned against it as pusillanimity. In introducing the *Spiritual Exercises*, he says, 'It will be very profitable for the one who is to go through the exercises to enter upon them with magnanimity and generosity.'

St Teresa said that mediocrity was the great obstacle to growth in holiness. Neither God nor man is served by the mediocre.

Christ the Lord seemed to have a special regard for passionate, whole-hearted people. He was so much more compassionate towards the woman taken in adultery and towards prostitutes that he was towards the legalistic Pharisees. He chose the hot-headed Peter to be his first pope, in spite of the fact that he had denied him three times. Paul was a man of total commitment, whether to persecuting Christ or to preaching him.

In Revelation 3:15, St John tells us, 'I know that you are neither hot nor cold. How I wish you were one or the other, hot or cold! But because you are lukewarm, neither hot nor cold, I will spew you out of my mouth! You keep saying, "I am so rich and secure I want nothing," Little do you realise how wretched you are, how pitiable and poor, how blind and naked! Take my advice … Whatever is dear to me I reprove and chastise. Be earnest about it.'

We need to be earnest about it, reproving and chastising our dear ego and this is what we do in meditation. We need to be earnest enough to start and then we need to be earnest enough to persevere. Saying the Mantra is like weeding a garden. As we say it, we push back the frontiers of the ego. But the forces of the ego, like the weeds, quickly recover and make another onslaught. That is why we have to meditate every day for the rest of our lives. The weeds, the energy of the ego, keep reforming. This is a fact of gardening and a fact of life. We must just accept it and deal with it. We should not be discouraged by our apparent failure to say the Mantra and keep out distraction. We say the Mantra not to be successful but to be faithful. Our obsession with success, which we learn from the world in which we live, is one of our greatest obstacles to perseverance in prayer. Yet 'spiritual success', if one had it, would be an almost insurmountable obstacle to spiritual growth!

Put it this way. After a thirty-minute period of meditation you have to say to the Lord, 'Sorry, I goofed that one again. Was I even a minute saying the Mantra? Help me to do better the next time.' You certainly will not leave with a bloated ego. On the other hand, supposing you could say to the Lord, 'Well that was a smashing meditation. I was bull'seye on the Mantra from start to finish. I pity those people who do not find saying the Mantra dead easy.' Do I hear echoes of the Gospel story in Luke 18, of the two men who went up to the temple to pray, the one a Pharisee and the other a tax-collector?

So apparent failure is no excuse for not continuing to meditate every day, twice a day, and for not starting again every time we become aware of distraction.

We discover through experience that being restricted to the Mantra leads to depth and breath in all dimensions of life. As we become committed to the Mantra we become deeper people, we become more absorbed and committed to everything that we do, solitude replaces loneliness, depth replaces shallowness, joy replaces listlessness.

There can be no trying out of meditation just to say that we know what it is. We must know what it is from experience and then we will know that we must be committed to it.

Meditation and Low Self-image

Some years ago during a mission, I was housed in the Home Economics Department of a Barrio school. One day I overheard the class being conducted next door – maybe for my benefit. It went something like this:

Teacher: 'The nose of the American is …?'
Courageous Student: 'Long.'
Teacher: 'Wrong! It's tall! The nose of the Filipino is …?'
Courageous Student: 'Small.'
Teacher: 'Wrong! It's flat!'

As I listened I squirmed as the self-image of those children was being squashed. First there were implications of inferiority on the basis of nationality and physique. Then the poor kids that had some initiative were clobbered because they did not give the rote answer expected by the teacher. No wonder these children will grow up with a low self-image. They are, in effect, being reared into a culture of shame. This is different from a guilt culture, where it is more important to live up to one's internal value system. In a shame culture, it is more important for me to be thought well of by you than for me to think well of myself. From earliest childhood, children are manipulated to conform because of shame. This often means that a price has to be paid for love. So often the child is told that it will get a reward if it is good, or if it achieves well. Its self worth is pegged to its achievements. Its being, of itself, has no value. From the earliest age, children are subjected to stroking exercises. We have graduations from kindergarten on and everyone has to get some kind of recognition. We do our best to develop sensitive, greedy egos.

As a consequence, children grow up very sensitive and competitive. The words and looks and even the imagined thoughts of others control them. One of the high values of the shame culture is smooth interpersonal relationships, so people hide feelings, and pay a big price because these feelings are often converted into psychosomatic sicknesses like high-blood pressure, asthma, allergy, ulcers. People may be psychologically mangled but cannot express it. They carry with them the hurts of their past lives. They are still shrivelled up inside because of the way they had been treated by someone who may be already dead. Death destroys a

life but not relationships. An unhealthy relationship with someone in the past can still effect us even if that person is now dead.
So, people compete with one another in all sorts of extraordinary
ways. To live means to appear better than others. What we really
are, 'to be', is of no importance.

To have a low self-image is to be a slave of the opinions of others
and to put our destinies in the hands of those who have hurt us in
the past. 'If I had been given a good education ... If I had been
loved as my other sisters were ... If I had a college degree ... if, if, if
... then I would be happy.' These ifs run through our lives. We are
slaves of the past, of our own sins and the sins of others.

It is rightly said, 'To err is human; to forgive divine.' All human
relationships are fraught with error and hurt. These hurts alienate
us from ourselves, from our centres. We do not want to be at our
centres because we feel that there is nothing lovable there. We are
like doughnuts – there is something running around outside but
there is no centre. Yet that centre is where our deepest being and
beauty is, this is where Christ is, this is where God is. This is where
the one who will enable us to forgive and to be alive again is.

We need to be restored to our own centres. To be able to enter
there, 'to be there,' to experience that it is an okay place to be.
When we are there the healing presence of Christ will enable us to
forgive.

When we say the Mantra we are there. We cannot continue to
pray the Mantra and be a victim of anger, hatred, and of all the
people in the past who have hurt us and destroyed our self-image.

One of our meditators shared about it in this way: 'When I first
tried to meditate I found myself wanting to run away. Then I realised that when I tried to meditate, my dis-ease came from the
fact that I hated my neighbour. I fought this and said that I would
try to see Christ in my neighbour. That was mission impossible!
My neighbour cheated and stole and used the vilest language
about us – Christ would never have done that. I continued to try to
meditate, putting aside the fidgeting and the distractions. Then it
seemed as if Christ from within said to me, "I am within. Look at
your neighbour with my eyes." I have tried to do that since then
and I now find myself a more free person. I can see and have compassion for the life history that crippled her. I even want to reach
out to help her.'

Meditation and Relationships

Jesus said to them,
'My solemn word is this. I am the sheep-gate.
All who came before me were thieves and marauders
whom the sheep did not heed.
I am the gate.
Whoever enters through me will be safe.
He will go in and out and find pasture.
The thief comes only to steal and slaughter and destroy.
I came that you may have life
and have it to the full.' (Jn 10:7-10)

A few years ago, *Time* magazine had a cover story on stress. It showed how this was a major problem in the world today. It told of how stress-relieving chemicals were a multimillion industry. It listed the many causes of stress – loss of job, moving residence, etc.. But then it told of one man who had all the causes – he had lost his job and changed his house six times in six years, yet he showed little signs of stress. When asked why, he answered, 'Maybe it is because I have a good wife and I go to Church on Sunday.'

Internal empowerment is an in-word at the present time. What empowers people, energises them, what makes people alive? 'I have a good wife and I go to Church on Sundays' seems to be the key – relationships. The person who has healthy and wholesome relationships seems to have more joy and energy and resilience in dealing with life's ups and downs.

We all have four main relationships, our relationship to ourselves, to others, to the world and to God. We tend to act the same way in all of these four dimensions of relationship. If we are critical or resentful towards others, we will tend to be critical and resentful also towards God. We will also have a hard time in accepting ourselves. When Jesus says that 'he came that we may have life and have it to the full' (Jn 10:10), I think that he wanted to improve all of these relationships.

In another place he tells us that 'the truth will set you free.' (Jn 8:32) We need to have a passion for the truth if we are to be energised by the Lord. The passion for the truth means that we need to face up to reality with honesty and humour. Freedom comes from facing up to reality, from accepting gracefully what is inevitable.

Most of our unfreedoms come from refusing to accept things just as they are. We have great plans for God, we know exactly what he should do, and he does not do it, and so we are frustrated that he has not become our servant. We know exactly what our neighbours should do, but they do not do it. We let this affect our moods and send our blood pressure soaring. We have great expectations of ourselves, we daydream ourselves into all kinds of successes that never happen, and are disgusted with ourselves as a result. So, myself and others and God all become very disappointing.

We will probably express the disappointment with others, and cover up the disappointment with ourselves and God, in different kinds of frenetic activity. We get out of relationship with ourselves because we do not find ourselves a nice place to be.

But inside ourselves is a nice place to be. When we learn to be still, within ourselves, with others, and with God, wonderful things happen. As we are still with ourselves, the emotions that were clogged up at the doors of our hearts seem to be able to move in and out more freely. When we find that it is just okay to be within ourselves, we find that we can go deeper into our own resources.

Relationships with others also demand stillness. We need the ability to be with another without an agenda, without a purpose, just to enjoy oeing together. This is something that is getting more difficult in today's busy world. Yet there cannot be relationships without wasting time together.

And then we must be still if we are to 'know that I am God.' (Ps 46) It is in stillness that we realise relatedness with God, that we are his creatures and that 'Even if a mother were to forget her child, never would I forget you.' (Is 49:15)

Stillness enables us to accept reality with honesty and humour. Humour is the ability to see the twist, the unexpected angle in a situation and to be able to enjoy it. Humour does not necessarily mean boisterous laughter but the 'chuckle in the gut,' the joy of living that comes from being at home within yourself. Meditation brings this kind of joy, and where this joy is, there is also an abundance of energy. Meditation can be the gateway into fullness of life. Once we relate to the Lord in stillness, we will find that all of our relationships will begin to improve.

Meditation and the Bogus

There is evidence that the founder of a prestigious world-wide Catholic Lay Movement organised the process for his own canonisation after his death. Fr Furneiss, of my own Redemptorist Congregation, was famous in England in the nineteenth century for his ministry to children. The evidence now seems to be that his work for children was contrived to sustain his reputation in that area and did not spring from a genuine spirituality. Sometimes we hear of apparently good priests who are discovered to be leading double lives. I know of a reputable doctor who, when he went out of town to give a lecture, arranged with his secretary to call him twice during his speech, so that the audience would be impressed with his importance. We are always shocked when we discover the bogus, the phoney, the plastic.

But then one day we tumble to the bogus in ourselves!

Perhaps one of the greatest burdens that we have to carry in life is the image people have of us. It creates expectations and, if we are not careful, we can become slaves of these expectations. One of the most dangerous 'images' is that of 'being holy.' We can be forced to live out of that image, that holiness, and become a slave to it. That is why religion that is too much on the surface is seldom deep. People who have a reputation for holiness and who appeal too easily to discernment and the 'will of God' as a reason for their actions can be escaping the relationship with God found in everyday life and in human situations. They can be bogus.

The world may be divided into two classes of people – the bad bad people and the good bad people. The bad bad people would be those like the younger son in the story of the forgiving father (Luke 15). He knew he was bad and had no problem in admitting it. The good bad people, would be similar to the older son, obedient, respectful, but resentful and lacking in compassion, a bogus person. Here are two big surprises: firstly, the Lord had much more time and compassion for the bad bads than for the good bads. Secondly, the people who come to meditation groups are much more likely to be good bad people than bad bad people!

I know from personal experience that a lot of the depression experienced by religious people springs from jealousy. Jealousy is an insidious vice that is very hard to admit, especially for one who is known to be holy or in a state of holiness. I remember a teacher telling me once that he taught many people how to play the guitar but none of them excelled. This was because he always kept something back, because he feared to have a rival to his own prowess as the best player in the establishment.

The Enneagram shows that each of us has some quality that we seek compulsively – being right, helpful, successful, special, wise, loyal, fun loving, strong or calm. If my self-esteem depends on my being wise or right or successful – or holy – I have a vested interest in your being stupid or wrong or a failure – or being sinful. As we grow up we learn that it is not socially acceptable to show ourselves for what we are in the raw, so we do it subtly. We often do or say one thing when our meaning or purpose may be quite contrary. We become bogus.

Now the Mantra is the great diagnose-er and the great cure for the bogus within us. As we say the Mantra, we are learning to sit at our own centre where Christ is. He is the Spirit of truth, the truth that sets us free. In his light, the bogus very quickly stands out. At first it makes us very uncomfortable. We want to stop meditation and to run away from truth and the light. But if we stick with the Mantra the ego is gradually unhooked and we can face the truth about ourselves and that truth will set us free.

There is a story about a man who had a very bad stutter. He never remembered when he had spoken a straight sentence. One day he found himself on a bus without any money. Stuck for a way to solve his predicament, he decided to exaggerate his stutter when the conductor came, in the hope that he would pass him by in exasperation. To his own amazement, the stutterer spoke his first straight sentence when the conductor came to him. For the first time he had accepted his stutter and the acceptance had freed him from it.

As we meditate we will more and more discover the bogus in ourselves, the venality, the dishonesty, the lustfulness that we are still capable of, in spite of the holy image that we project before others. As we say the Mantra we will become more free to accept the darker side of ourselves and, once we have accepted it, it looses control over us. We become more integrated and less bogus.

Meditation and Purity of Passion

My first teacher in meditation used to say that if you have any expectations in prayer and they are not fulfilled then you got what you deserve. I came to meditation with some expectations. I remember hearing the German Redemptorist moral theologian, Fr Bernard Häring, a palpably contemplative man, say that if you fly off the handle you are not yet contemplative. So I expected that meditation would bring a great calm, a dulling of passion.

On the contrary, in my own experience, and in the experience of those on the way of meditation that I have listened to, it seems that almost the opposite is true. When one begins to meditate one becomes more aware of sensuality, greed, jealousy, anger. There can be a new discomfort of wrestling within.

It took me some time to understand what was happening. What was happening, I think, was a simplification, a purification, a separation of passion. As one meditates one extricates the ego from what one is feeling and so feels the feeling more purely. This is a very freeing experience but at first it can be frightening. Let me explain it in this way. A friend of mine told me, 'I had a great relationship with my father but when he died I got over it fairly easily. I had a terrible relationship with my mother but when she died I was in pieces for years.'

How explain the difference? In her relationship with her father there was no hurt ego and so she could let go of the relationship fairly easily. But in her relationship with her mother there was a mangled ego and the process of extricating herself from it was, of course, excruciatingly painful.

When we begin to meditate we begin to unhook the ego from its attachments and this can often be frightening. It can challenge us to stand on our own feet in the face of peer pressure. Meditators report this process in very simple, as well as very demanding, areas. One says, 'Before I began to meditate I used to spend a lot on make-up and manicures. Now I do not feel any need for these things. But sometimes I am still afraid of what my friends will think.' Another says, 'I am beginning to realise that I am very unfair to the people working for me. But I am afraid of the price of justice.' Yet another says, 'I must have been repressing this all along but now I see clearly that I am in love with a married man. It frightens me to have to face this truth and deal with it maturely.' The little Mantra is really mischievous. It forces us to be honest even if we do not want to be.

Our feelings towards any person, object or event can be very confused or ambivalent. Confused or ambivalent feelings are usually the results of complication because of our egos. As we meditate we begin to detach from our egos. This is a necessary step to come to freedom and clarity but it is a step that is at first frightening. It is said that Mahatma Gandhi's power lay in the fact that he had perfectly aligned his sexuality, his ambition and his anger. These are powerful emotions that can be highly destructive if allowed to act blindly at the bidding of the ego. But if these emotions are purified they can be reservoirs of energy for good. Chastity is when the energies of love are directed to another. When sought for themselves, they became lust.

When we observe Christ we notice how calm he was in the face of personal affront. Even when he was challenged to prove himself, mocked, rejected in favour of a criminal, or spat upon, he did not react. But he was very angry when he saw his house – the temple and the little ones – desecrated. Christ showed plenty of passion but it was pure passion. It was passion not in response to a hurt ego but in response to seeing the image of his father trampled on by the self-righteous.

If we are to be disciples of Christ we need to be detached from our egos. We need to be aware of our passions, our loves, our urges. We need to be able to distinguish what is serving false reality, the ego, and what is serving the true reality, God. The best way that I know to bring this detachment about is the way of the Mantra.

When we say the Mantra we are in neutral gear before God. I notice that when my motorcycle is not well tuned it will run only when revved up. At traffic lights I will have to keep it revved or it will cut out. Sometimes I have to rev it against the breaks. This is what happens when our egos are fighting against our passions. There is a lot of noise and activity and a great waste of energy. This has to be maintained to avoid extinction. A mechanic tunes an engine when it is idle, just purring over. When we say the Mantra we are in neutral and fully alert. We are ready to move easily and effectively into gear. Our silence prepares us for efficient service.

Meditation and Transcendence

There was a time when people would ask a priest, 'Is such and such a sin?' or 'How far can I go without committing sin?' and the priest would give a detailed and exact reply. If asked today, the priest might answer, 'What do you think yourself? What would be the most responsible or the most mature or the most transcending thing to do?'

What is maturity anyhow? One description of it is to have consistency between the physical, social and transcendent parts of our human make up. Let's try to chew that mouthful a little!

The newly born baby is totally body. Its main preoccupation is its physical needs – food, warmth, cuddling. Its happiness is in fulfilling these and avoiding physical pain. Self is the source of pleasure. It can only value others as objects or sources of pleasure.

Gradually the child learns that its mother and others can be more than pleasure objects. Social contact has a meaning in itself. Pleasure also comes from acceptance, friendship, recognition, communication, complementarity. The other is more than an object, and becomes a person. Sexuality is more than something physical; it is social and pertains to relationships. Pain can be emotional, springing from failure in relationships, as well as from unfulfiled physical needs.

The human person is also capable of thinking and judging. The human person can have values that transcend what is just physical or social. The person can reach out to friendships that are mutually beneficial, or even to benevolence and disinterested love. The values of honesty, justice, chastity can enable the human person to rise above his or her self. Pain can be moral, from seeing things that are not as they should be.

For those with a religious perspective, this may be called a response to God or 'religion'. There are many people seeking transcendence in today's world while rejecting the organised expressions of religion. It is important not to underestimate this as it is a valid, and often very elevating, relationship with 'the one beyond,' even if not explicitly acknowledged as such.

We are acting maturely when there is consistency between the three levels within us. It is desirable and necessary for our growth that we enjoy the physical. Our bodies can and should be sources of pleasure to us. Seeing, eating, touching, smelling, hearing, sports, the exercise of our sexuality, are given to us for enjoyment. But the enjoyment is mature only when it is consistent with our values. These will vary from person to person. What might be quite mature and consistent with values for a married couple may be immature or destructive for someone who is not married. The eating and drinking that is mature for the ordinary person might be quite immature for the alcoholic or diabetic.

Social interaction with the same and the opposite sex is something that can and should be enjoyed. However, when this interaction transgresses values it is no longer mature. When we dominate, exploit, degrade, manipulate or seduce others, we have eliminated the transcendent dimension.

It is of some value to know where we stand in the matter of maturity. One of the simplest tests for finding this out is to look at our prayer life. If, when you try to pray, you are blocked or constantly distracted by physical concerns (food, sex, comfort, wealth) then you may be fixated at the physical level. If, on the other hand, the block or the preoccupation is with your social relationships and your hurts and dependencies on others, it is likely that you are fixated on the social. But if you are more concerned with presence to the Lord and bringing the needs of others and of the world into that presence, it is probable that the transcendent is predominating in your life. Meditating, praying the Mantra, is a way of transcending all fixation and of becoming detached day by day from the compulsive behaviour that it causes.

What causes fixation, the inability to transcend? Generally a childhood experience of deprivation. Bodily deprivation, deprivation of food and warmth, and of objects considered important, may cause the development of the acquisitive fixations. Deprivation of physical warmth and cuddling may cause a fixation about physical touch or sexuality. Not being appreciated, affirmed, loved, may cause a craving for social approval in its myriad forms. Cravings carry with them the fear of not acquiring the object craved for. Our deprivations – and all of us have them – lead to self-centredness, ego-centredness, and the inability to transcend self.

Psychology and psychotherapy offer their solutions. They sometimes help and sometimes fail. The simple saying of the Mantra is,
in my experience and in the Christian tradition, a time-tested
means of detaching the ego from the self, and so of setting one free
to become transcendent.

Meditation, Death and Resurrection

Death and birth are very closely related. Every death is a birth and every birth is a death. If the child in the womb were able, it would resist birth. It fears the cold outside world and does not want to enter into it. Every birth is, in a sense, premature; we are never ready for the cold world. We are never quite ready for the next stage. The child is never quite ready to go to school. Later the same child is not ready to leave school and go into the competitive world. Getting married, too, or choosing a profession is a birth for which we are never fully prepared.

Each of these births is also a death. When a child is born it dies to its past existence in the womb. When it goes to school it dies to its security in the home. Life is a series of births and deaths, and of deaths and resurrections.

There is always some pain in birth as there is in death. The degree of pain depends on the clinging. If there is much clinging, if there is a resistance to letting go, the wrenching is greater.

The clinging does not necessarily indicate love. It is easier to let go of the loved than of the unloved. When the loved person or object is taken away there is a vacuum but that can easily be filled again. But when the unloved person goes there is a wrenching. Parts of our crushed egos are still entangled in that person or object. We may have been dependent on the person who died and we are now angry or afraid when they have left us. Generally we do not mourn for the other person. We mourn mostly for ourselves. The lives of many are stunted by anger towards a parent who died young and failed to provide fully for them. Just recently I attended a deathbed where a daughter shouted at her dead father, 'How dare you die after all the money we spent on you?' A legitimate feeling that society rarely lets one express!

John Main used to call meditation the first death which prepares us for the second death, the physical death. He also said that a life that is a preparation for death is a sad life. This life is a preparation for a new life, for life more fully with God, for resurrection. If clinging is what makes death hard to accept then the twice daily practice of meditation is a great preparation for it. Meditation detaching us daily from everything – from words, thoughts, self-centredness, from the ego. As we meditate we become light and free. We become free to let others enter new life and to enter it ourselves.

In daily life we go through little deaths which take us through the five stages of dying enumerated by Dr Elizabeth Kübler-Ross. According to her, the first reaction to the possibility of death is denial: it could not be me, there must be a mistake! Then comes anger: how could God do this to me?, the doctors and the nurses are stupid! Then there is bargaining: I will build a church if you will make me well. The fourth stage is characterised by depression. Then one may finally come to acceptance.

The discipline of the Mantra exercises our ability to let go as we experience our little deaths in daily life. The little deaths may be our failures, or the realisation of our own selfishness or limitation. We go through the five steps of dying in coping with these. If we have been doing this we will be better prepared to accept death itself when it comes.

The practice of meditation prepares us for death and dying also in another way. One of the fears of the aging is that their lives will no longer be useful and that they will have nothing worthwhile to contribute as they grow older. If during one's active days one has come to appreciate prayer and make it – as John Main did – 'the axis on which my day was built,' then one learns to look forward to old age for the leisure it will allow one for one's most valued and favoured activity.

Each time we meditate we enter the passion of Jesus. As he handed himself and all that he was into the hands of the Father so do we every time we leave self behind and say our Mantra. As the Father accepted the oblation of Christ and restored him to life, we too are led in our meditation to a new fullness of life, to resurrection.

We fear 'Goodbyes' and the separation that they bring about. But if we are sure of Christ's presence with us now, his indwelling presence, there is no leaving at death, there is only a movement into a different mode of that presence. There is nothing to fear because there is no goodbye.

I can remember the final watch as my father died. Some people were coping by being fussy and busy. This included pushing prayers upon the dying man and on one another. I just silently said the Mantra. I was in his presence. My father was moving into a new intensity of that presence.

What more was there to say?

Service

Silence into Service

Two disciples went to the Master and asked him for the secret of holiness. The Master said, 'Wait,' and walked away.

After an agitated week, one of them came back to the Master and said, 'Master what is the secret of holiness?'
The Master again said, 'Wait, send me your companion.'
The other disciple came to the Master and asked,
'Is there something else, Master?'
'No,' the Master replied.

The heart of the Gospel is love, a love that is shown by service. Jesus said, 'I have come, not to be served, but to serve.' The great obstacle to loving service is impatience. The great remedy for impatience is silence and the persistent saying of the Mantra.

Some of the great attitudes of love are:
> 'I will hear your story so that I can know who you are.'
> 'I will help you give birth to yourself.'
> 'I will be for you whatever you need me to be.'

It is often difficult to listen to another's story. We want to jump ahead or fix it right away, to tell the other – whether the other be a person or a group or a community – what he or she or they should do or should have done. In this way we block rather that hasten the liberation of the other. If we truly love we will have patience. We will let ourselves appear stupid to those who would be threatened by our wisdom. We will appear to have forgotten, to those who do not need to be reminded of what they are not ready to recall. We will be in no hurry for those whose utterances are punctuated by long periods of silence. We will be open beside those who pour out their hearts like a dam that is bursting.

We will accept abuse knowing that it is displaced. The anger we hear hitting us is often anger directed to some unidentified target in the past. If we love, we take the anger, and when we have taken it, pressure is released. Thus, the other may be able to feel God's love through our loving.

The core of all ministry is story-listening. This is being able to listen to others talk about their pain. Stories start the minister off where the person or the people are. The great paradigm of this kind of ministry is the Melon Story.

There was a land in which the people believed that a melon was a monster. When they discovered one, while harvesting or hunting, they skirted it in fear. A son of that land went to a high-class university and, of course, learned that a melon was not a monster. When he returned home on vacation, he joined his relatives in reaping the harvest. The cry 'monster' was heard and everyone ran except for the learned one from the university. He laughed and walked up to the melon. He picked it up, slashed it into slices and began to eat it. He walked back to the people, full of satisfaction with his performance. But he was amazed, for now they were running from him. They were saying, 'If he can do that to the monster, what a monster he himself must have become.'

Later, another son went to a less distinguished seat of learning. There he also learned that a melon was not a monster. When he returned, he too went harvesting with the others. When the cry 'monster' was heard, he forgot all about what he had learned and ran with the others. Then he began to remember that he had learned that a melon was not a monster, so he asked, 'Why are we running?' He was told, 'From the melon monster, of course.' He then asked, 'How do we know that the melon is a monster?'

After hours of trying, nobody could give a satisfactory answer. So they were willing to take another look at the 'monster'. They looked at it from afar, then they prodded it with a long bamboo, and eventually they touched it, sliced it and ate it up.

It was a slow process, a patient process, a process that went with the pace of the people. It was a process that eventually worked.

The great obstacle to this process is our impatience. We tell ourselves that we have other things to do. This person is too demanding. These people are stupid. They lack education. They lack faith. I have heard it all before and to no avail. This obstacle cannot be removed by steeling our wills and saying, 'I will make myself sit and listen.' When we try to do this we find our legs walking away before we realise it, or our thoughts wandering to the place where we would prefer to be.

We find the process of patient active listening difficult because of the impatience that is within ourselves. In meditation we experience this very impatience. Saying the Mantra is such a simple matter and yet we fail. Impatience tends to make us respond with violence or abandonment. We tend to try to grasp the Mantra by an act of the will and hold it in place no matter what. But distractions come, and like a slippery eel, the Mantra slips out of our grasp. As we repeat the process, our anger and impatience may build up. Then we may decide to abandon the Mantra altogether. That is the final impatience.

Or we can be patient and persistent. We can lay the Mantra back on our consciousness with the gentleness of returning a phonograph needle on to a record. We do this with perseverance, with persistence, but never with impatience. As we do this we reconcile two opposite poles within ourselves.

Then we find that, without noticing it, this reconciliation of opposites, this patience and persistence, overflows into our ministry. Our silence has disposed us for effective service and ministry.

Meditation
and Community-Making

On the evening of the first day of the week, even though the disciples had
locked the doors of the place where they were for fear of the Jews, Jesus
came and stood before them.
'Peace be with you,' he said.
When he had said this he showed his hands and his side. At the sight of the
Lord the disciples rejoiced.
'Peace be with you,' he said again.
'As the Father has sent me, so I send you.'
Then he breathed on them and said:
'Receive the Holy Spirit.
If you forgive men's sins, they are forgiven;
If you hold them bound, they are held bound.' (Jn 20:19-23)

In the meditation groups that I have been associated with, the
question always comes up at the beginning: Why should I be with
these people? We have nothing in common socially, economically
or in temperament? They will not understand my problems.

After a few months of praying the Mantra, these questions cease
to bother anyone. A bond is formed, a maturation takes place, and
the expectation about solving problems changes.

Experience shows how unifying silence is. If a director and di-
rectee can spend time in silence together before a spiritual direction session it gives a new richness to the sharing. So too, if priests
in a deanery or vicariate, or religious in their community, can
spend time together in silence before a meeting, there is a greater
chance that the meeting will be fruitful. When Pope John Paul II
invited leaders of the world religions to meet at Assisi, the only
certainly unifying prayer that they could use was silence.

This matter of community is essential for all of us, whether we are
in religious communities, in families, or in places of work. From
time to time we will come across people – often very good people
– who will get under our skins, make us angry or bring out the
worst in us. G. K. Chesterton once said that families are common-
ly held to be havens of love in oceans of hate. The opposite, he

said, is often true. Families are havens of hate in an ocean of bogus love. When we are with outsiders we can maintain pretences of peace, but in the close community of the family, or work-place, or the religious house, that is not always possible.

Most of the problems spring from our own egos. Consciously or unconsciously, there is a program within us of how others should act and particularly how they should act towards us. For example, in the prayers in my religious community we sometimes say the verses of the Psalms one after another. I remember feeling very angry one morning when someone led the prayers in an anti-clockwise rather than a clockwise direction. Why not? Apart from my inbuilt programming? Two good people can irritate each other so much. One may be big and expansive, the other meticulous and exact. Their actuations can annoy one another no end.

All these things are attributes of the person. Beneath all of these is a weak, poor, insecure human person. When we come in touch with that person we immediately become more tolerant, more compassionate, more free from the domination of the actuations and attributes of others. When we let go of our own need to dominate and manipulate, we become more tolerant of the other. Tolerance will quickly yield to acceptance of the other and the right of the other to be different. This acceptance may yield to affirmation and the realisation that the other's 'being different' is something complementary and that, if acknowledged, it can even be an enrichment to us.

If we are surprised that there is disruption in our communities, we have not read the gospels well. Jesus was the leader and novice master of the apostles. Yet what intrigue and dishonesty and human frailty there was amongst them! James and John were always seeking the inside track in favours with the Lord, making the others angry over this. Peter was an intolerable braggart and the treacherous Judas turned Jesus in. Christ was right in the middle of this mess!

The scene in John 20, where Christ meets the apostles after the resurrection, is a very powerful one. Jesus had disappointed them. They had expected him to be a political saviour who would drive out the Romans and in whose government they would have high places. However, instead of being lifted up on a throne in victory he was lifted up on a cross as a failure. They too had failed him ter-

ribly. They had fallen asleep when he had asked them to watch
while he prayed, Judas had betrayed him, Peter had denied him,
and all ran away except John. They must have been tense as he
now appeared before them. They had every reason to expect him
to reprimand and reject them. But what did Jesus say? 'Shalom!
Peace be with you.' he breathed on them and said, 'Receive the
Holy Spirit. When you forgive sins they are forgiven; when you
retain sins they are retained.' What he seemed to say was this,
'Look here, men, there is a lot of hurt between us but life must go
on and we must work together. I know that forgiveness is beyond
your power. To err is human, to forgive is divine. So I am giving
you my Spirit to empower you to forgive. Now if you forgive, that
is the end of it. If you choose not to forgive, you continue to carry
the poison of the hurts within you.' He empowered them to forgive, that they may set themselves and others free, but he does not
force them.

This is the first apostolate for all of us. Learning to be at least tolerant, if not accepting and affirming, of those who irritate or hurt us,
especially those who are around us all the time. Without this atti-
tude, option for the poor and commitment to the people 'out
there' is just a pious dream or a form of escapism.

The wisdom of the East has always held that one cannot be silent
and angry at the same time. In silence the psyche is enabled to cast
off what is poisonous to it. As still water lets straw float to the surface and heavier material sink, so too we become clearer and un-
clogged, freed from anger, as we enter into silence.

The discipline of the Mantra, and the silence towards which it
brings us, is a discipline which makes us hold on in love, in spite
of our tensions. When the storm passes over, calm is restored. The
twice daily saying of the Mantra establishes this calm as habitual,
and with it brings great benefits to both body and soul.

It is from the stillness within that we most effectively and lovingly
reach out to others and to the other. The human person is like a
bowl: if it is full of anger and hate, it can only give out anger and
hate. If it is full of love, it can only give love. As the Mantra brings
us to stillness, it brings us to love. When we are still within, we can
be with ourselves in tolerance and love. When we can be with ourselves in tolerance and love, we can also be with others in the same
way.

Prayer groups begin with persons. The group comes together because of the attraction or reputation of the leader or because
friends invite one another. This is a very normal way of coming
into discipleship. But as time goes on, persons fade and the Person
becomes important. As the prayer group develops, the person of
Christ rather than any human person becomes the centre and the
attraction. When we realise that he is the centre, he whose Spirit is
the enabler of forgiveness, all other persons, no matter how su-
perficially repulsive, fit into the family of love.

Meditation
and the Option for the Poor

Jesus, full of the Holy Spirit, then returned from the Jordan and was conducted by the Spirit into the desert for forty days, where he was tempted by the devil. During that time he ate nothing, and at the end of it he was hungry. The devil said to him, 'If you are the Son of God, command this stone to turn into bread.' Jesus answered him, 'Scripture has it, "Not on bread alone shall man live."'

Then the devil took him up higher and showed him all the kingdoms of the world in a single instant. He said to him, 'I will give you all this power and the glory of these kingdoms: the power has been given to me and I give it to whomever I wish. Prostrate yourself in homage before me, and it shall all be yours.' In reply, Jesus said to him, 'Scripture has it, "You shall do homage to the Lord your God; him alone shall you adore."'

Then the devil led him to Jerusalem, set him on the parapet of the temple and said to him, 'If you are the Son of God, throw yourself down here, for Scripture has it, "He will bid his angels to watch over you"; and again, "With their hands they will support you, that you may never stumble on a stone."'

Jesus said to him in reply, "It also says, "You shall not put the Lord your God to the test."'

When the devil had finished all the tempting he left him, to await another opportunity.

Jesus returned in the power of the Spirit to Galilee, and his reputation grew throughout the region. He was teaching in their synagogues, and all were loud in his praise.

He came to Nazareth where he had been reared, and entering the synagogue on the sabbath, as he was in the habit of doing, he stood up to do the reading. When the book of the prophet Isaiah was handed him, he unrolled the scroll and found the passage where it was written:
'The spirit of the Lord is upon me;
Therefore he has anointed me.
He has sent me to bring glad tidings to the poor,
to proclaim liberty to captives,
Recovery of sight to the blind
and release to prisoners,
To announce a year of favour from the Lord.' (Lk 4:1-18)

Recently I got a card from a friend which said, 'May you have success and all the things that you need to make you happy.' It was a nice summary of the values of this world with which we are all imbued. We see happiness as coming from things and achievements, whereas real happiness comes only from the transcendence of our desires, ambitions and needs.

It is consoling to see that Christ himself had to struggle with these temptations. In chapter four of the gospel of St Luke we have a beautiful psycho-drama which portrays the interior struggle of Jesus. This should not be read separately from the following verses where he enters the synagogue and makes, as it were, his mission statement.

The first temptation is to change stones into bread. Jesus is tempted not to accept the limitation of being human but to use his 'Godness' to achieve possessions in a short-cut way. It is basically a temptation to short-circuit the plan of the Father and not to accept the poverty of being human. This temptation to short-circuit the plan of the Father and to seek possessions by fair means or foul is very obvious in the world around us. It is also evident in our spiritual lives. We may have given up material greed but we substitute spiritual acquisitiveness. We strive for security in spiritual experiences, virtue, or even in the knowledge that we are good at praying. But to follow Christ we have to leave self behind, and that includes spiritual selfishness.

The second temptation is to power. 'Prostrate yourself in homage before me and this shall all be yours.' It is very hard to gain power in the world without bowing down to Satan. If some have done so, it is hard for them to stay on in power without bowing to the devil. The Christian way is the way of powerlessness and dependence on God. The model for Christ's kingdom was not power over others, but the helplessness of the little child. Hunger for power is also apparent in the world around us and in the spiritual life. There is a great danger in prayer-forms that give us power over others. The power to draw crowds, or to elicit tears, or confessions, or speaking in tongues or miracles of healing. When these gifts are given they are to be accepted with gratitude, but there is great danger in having the power to elicit them. If we exercise power over religious experience we will inevitably be tempted to exercise power over God himself. Scripture shows that God will not be controlled either by our good deeds or our bad ones. Our good deeds will not force him to cuddle us or our bad deeds force him to punish us. Total powerlessness before God is the only strength of the Christian.

Finally, Satan tempted Jesus to jump from the temple and win the adulation of the crowds. Several times Jesus was challenged to prove by a sign that he was the Messiah. On the cross he was also challenged by the crowd: 'Come down from the cross and we will believe.' The chief priests, and in Matthew's account, even the two who were crucified with him, joined in challenging him to prove himself. This temptation is also prevalent in the world. Success and the symbols of success enslave so many. In the Church, too, we have the scandal of the misuse of ecclesiastical prestige symbols and titles. In our own prayer perhaps our greatest obstacle is our obsession with success. We want to be able to show off, at least to ourselves, that we are good at prayer. If we are distracted, we are disgusted with ourselves and think that our prayer is of no value. We cannot display it before God and say, 'Thank God I am not like the others.' But in the gospels it was not the one who used these words who went home justified!

After the temptations, Jesus went back to Nazareth where he was reared, back to his roots. There he took the book of the prophet Isaiah and read from it:
'He has sent me to bring glad tidings to the poor,
Liberty to captives,
Recovery of sight to the blind
and release to prisoners.'

This was his mission, this is our mission.

We are called by Christ, and by his Church today, to make an option for the poor. The perspectives and the welfare of the deprived must be ours. If we are to be ministers of Christ, and this is a challenge to every Christian, we must be free within, free from the urgings of the ego for possessions, power and prestige. We need poverty within.

I know no better way to prepare to follow Christ in poverty, humility and powerlessness, than the discipline of the twice daily saying of the Mantra.

Meditation and Apostolate

He proposed still another parable: 'The reign of God is like a mustard seed which someone took and sowed in his field. It is the smallest seed of all, yet when full grown it is the largest of plants. It becomes so big a shrub the birds of the sky come and build their nests in its branches.'

He offered them still another image: 'The reign of God is like yeast which a woman took and kneaded into three measures of flour. Eventually the whole mass of dough began to rise.' (Mt 13:31-33)

There is a story about a little boy who went into a sculptor's workshop. He saw a big rock there. A month later when he came back he saw a huge stone lion where the rock had been. He asked the sculptor in amazement, 'Sir, how did you know that there was a lion inside that rock?' The sculptor pondered for a while and said, 'Maybe I was able to see the lion in the rock because I first saw him in my own heart.'

Apostolate is seeing Christ in all things and in all people. But we cannot see him outside ourselves unless we have seen him first in our own hearts.

Laurence Freeman tells a very striking story about a sister who worked for thirty years in India. One day she mentioned something about prayer to an Indian friend. Her Indian friend looked back in surprise and said, 'Are you Christians religious people? We see your schools and your hospitals and your various activities but we do not see you as religious or spiritual people.'

Why has our Church come to stand for things and achievements rather than for presence and vision?

I believe that the problem lies mainly within us, where the treasure also lies. If we are full of our own ego, our apostolic work will merely be projections of our own selves. Many of our churches and church buildings may actually be sins against chastity. Those who have chosen celibacy, seeing that they cannot live on in their children, procreate a building or some edifice by which, in some neurotic way, they believe they can live on. Thus we build churches instead of Church.

The worldly desire for power, possessions and prestige – no less

common among Church people than among others – are enemies
of building up the kingdom. Clergy and religious people can be
great bullies. We can use the respect that the people give us to get
away with conduct that is not tolerated in secular society. We can
jump the queue; we can give figures to justify our projects that are
dishonest, we can call people to 'discuss' a project that we have already decided on; we can use people shamelessly. People let us
get away with it because of who we are. They capitulate to our
being overbearing. We are the ones that suffer – our egos are in-
flated by our pillage of the kingdom.

A great paradigm of false and true ministry is found in two little
parables in Matthew 13:31-33. The first one may be retold like this:
'The pastoral agent can be like the mustard seed which someone
took and sowed in the field. It is the smallest seed of all, yet when
full grown it is the largest of plants. It becomes so big a shrub that
the birds of the air come and build their nests in its branches.' We,
little seeds, can easily make ourselves into big 'shrubs', not real
trees, through our ministry. We may want to be the generous
Santa Claus to whom people come with their requests. We can in
this way become big oak trees under which nothing else blooms.

The second parable may be interpreted in this way: 'The pastoral
agent can be like yeast which a woman took and kneaded into
three measures of flour. Eventually the mass of dough began to
rise.' Here we have an image of leadership where the growth of
the other is the objective, where the latent energies in the other are
released, where the beauty of the other is appreciated. In this process, the pastoral agent is learning from the ones served and being
evangelised in the serving. He or she learns that leadership is not
an exercise of power but rather of empowerment.

A ministry which ends in one's being acclaimed as a success is a
sign of one's having failed. Five hundred years before Christ the
Chinese philosopher Lao Tse saw this:

A leader is best
when people barely know he exists:
Not so good
when people obey and acclaim him;
worse when people despise him.
But of a good leader
who talks little,
when his work is done,

his aim fulfilled,
they will say
'We did it ourselves.'

This was the leadership of Christ himself. He achieved nothing. He ended his life in utter failure. Yet he empowered a Church that will endure to the end of time.

To be his apostles, facilitators of the growth of the seed that is already planted in our people, we have to be in constant struggle with the big obstacle, both corporately and personally, that stands in the way of his reign. That obstacle is the ego. We can so easily use our ministry to serve our ego, but when we do that we are prostituting the kingdom, we are serving a false God, we are living in unreality.

Ministry demands self-restraining love. It demands that one must ever strive to be what the other needs one to be. It demands the poverty of holding on to nothing for oneself that the other may grow. And the best training that I know in this kind of ministry or apostolate, is to say the Mantra every day, twice a day, for twenty to thirty minutes each time.

Meditation and Listening

Not finding Jesus, Mary and Joseph returned to Jerusalem in search of him. On the third day they came upon him in the temple, sitting in the midst of the teachers, listening to them and asking them questions. All who heard him were amazed at his intelligence and his answers. (Lk 2:45-47)

A little boy and his mother were in town for the day. They went into a restaurant for a snack. When the waiter came along the mother began to order, but the waiter noticed that the little boy wanted to say something.

'Let the little man tell us himself what he wants,' said the waiter.
'I'll have a ham-bur-ger,' said the little boy.
When the waiter went off to get the order, the little boy said,
'You know, Mommy, that man thinks I'm real.'

There is nothing more affirming than being heard. It is what gives one reality, a sense of who one is. There is nothing more painful than not being heard, not being understood, especially when one is trying to express one's deep feelings or hurts or needs. Just imagine saying to somebody, 'I am going in now to get the results of my tests. The doctor thinks I may have cancer,' and that other person replies, 'I hope the corner shop is open, I would like to buy cigarettes.'

John Main used to make the point that one of the great sufferings of Jesus was that people did not hear his great love for them. For example, at the Last Supper he was trying to share his love and the fear of his impending death with the disciples, but they were more concerned about who would be in the highest places in the kingdom.

If we look at the forms of apostolate that seem to be effective today, we will find that the key factor in them all is listening. There are now over two hundred programmes based on the insights of the Alcoholics Anonymous, Gamblers Anonymous, Overeaters Anonymous, Women Hurt by Abortion, etc.. One of the principal dynamics in all of these is being listened to by another so-called weak person who is not threatening. Likewise, listening is fundamental to Clinical Pastoral Education, Marriage Encounter, the *Spiritual Exercises* of St Ignatius and any form of Pastoral Counselling or Spiritual Direction.

If one is to be effective in ministry, the first requirement is positive regard and love for the people with whom one works. There is no better way of affirming people, and showing that love and positive regard, than by listening to them and showing that you have heard. A very frequent reason for our failure as pastors is that we fail to communicate our love to our people. One of the ways of doing this is to listen to them attentively. I once preached a sermon on 'The saints I've met recently.' I mentioned some people in the parish that I had encountered, people looking after the old and the sick and bearing all sorts of burdens. I was amazed at the positive reaction to the sermon. People felt very affirmed. As if they were saying, 'It is good to hear that you are hearing our lives.'

But we cannot be at home with others and listening to them unless there is stillness within ourselves. If we are not within ourselves, our minds will be running off in different directions. We will cut off the other when any matter is touched with which we are not comfortable.

It is impossible for us to communicate well to people if we have not listened to them. Our message can only touch people when they can hear their own experience in it. Good communication is to feed back in an organised way what people have said in a disorganised way. I have found that if I want to tune in to what is happening in the parish, it is very important to listen to everyone, but especially to those who are drunk or a little mentally unstable. They have less inhibitions and may give you the truth that you need to hear bluntly, if you have the ears to hear it.

Priests and religious are notoriously bad listeners. People look to us as having the answers, as knowing it all. We tend to accept and internalise that image and so we imagine that we do not need to listen.

Naturally, we cannot communicate the Lord to others, unless we have been listening to his message in his word and in silence. As we continue to say the Mantra and put aside distraction, God's word is active within our depths. When we come to speak we will often be surprised where the wisdom comes from.

The first time we hear of Jesus speaking, we hear of his wisdom and of his listening ability. When Mary and Joseph found him in the temple he was 'listening to them and asking them questions.' It was because he listened to them that the teachers heard him and were amazed by the wisdom of his answers.

Again and again in his ministry, we see Jesus listening to others and allowing, or even encouraging, them to express their pain and their need. Perhaps the greatest example of ministry through listening that Jesus gives us, is when he joins the disciples on the road to Emmaus after he has risen from the dead. The disciples were dejected, walking away from Jerusalem, the place of their failure and broken dreams. So depressed are they that they do not even recognise Jesus when he joins them. He asks them why they are sad. They answer, 'Are you the only one who does not know what happened?' 'What happened?' he asks. Then they tell him their story. After listening to them he points out to them what the Scriptures say about the Messiah and how he was destined to suffer. Thus they begin to see that another conclusion may be drawn from the facts. This is as it should be. Christ has indeed risen. The story of dejection becomes a story of hope. It was only when he had listened to them that they could hear him speak.

The Emmaus story is a model for our ministry. It is a model of listening in which we have to be trained. We have to be able to listen to another without distraction, without judgment or condemnation, without worrying about what our response will be, without being defensive, without intrusion by our egos and our personal agendas, trusting that the Lord will give us the appropriate response when it is needed. In praying the Mantra we are learning to 'let go' of all that is the product of our own ego. As we give our attention to the Mantra, listening to it sounding within ourselves, we also become more present to ourselves, to others and to God and more available to be his instruments.

Missionaries and Mothers-in-Law

About thirty years ago I left Ireland for the Philippines. At the same time my brothers were marrying and my mother was becoming a multiple mother-in-law. There are some parallels between what was happening to her, to me, and to the Church in those years.

My mother reared seven sons and helped my father build up his business. Her life was a busy challenging one in which she was fruitful, saw growth, saw results and was to a great extent in charge. She cared for her children who needed her and loved her in return. She was appreciated as a spouse and as a partner by my father.

But then things began to change. I left for 'the missions' and, one after the other, my brothers got married. Their wives would now be the centre of their lives. More professional people were brought in to handle the business. Suddenly she found herself in a new rôle; a rôle in which she was no longer at centre stage, a rôle in which there was much less action. It was a very delicate rôle. She had the wisdom of years of experience behind her but she had to learn to hold her advice. The young ones wanted to live their own lives in their own ways. She had to stand back and often see them make mistakes that could have been avoided had her advice been followed. She had to learn to distinguish between being helpful and interfering. An apparently innocent little remark could occasion a major falling out and a period of tension until reconciliation could again be forged. She often got caught between the joy of being useful and the oppression of being used. If asked to baby-sit she would wonder if she was being used or being useful.

But it was not without its joys. She could feel happy that her job was done. She could still feel a fruitfulness in her grandchildren and enjoy the female company of her daughters-in-law. She was looked up to by a broader family circle without having to take any responsibility for them.

My life paralleled hers. I grew up in the Church of Pope Pius XII. It was a triumphant Church that was confident that it had all the answers. It was an hierarchical Church where authority and wisdom came from above though very clear channels. It was a Church where the prevailing image of Christ was that of king. The Church sent out missionaries to win souls for Christ. They went out to conquer the darkness of paganism and to counter the blindness of Protestantism. They were bringers of life to the dead and light to the blind. This was the self image that I had as I sailed through the Suez Canal and across the Indian Ocean.

Then came the Second Vatican Council. The windows of the Church were opened by Pope John XXIII and gale force winds blew through the Church. All sorts of new strange-sounding phrases became popular. The Church is the People of God! We must listen to the signs of the times! Subsidiarity and co-responsibility became the ways of describing authority. The priesthood of the laity was to be recognised. The laity were to have their say and their rôles. We were called to be ecumenical and to realise that God could and did act through means other than the Holy Roman Catholic Church. Mission was not to bring light but to discover the light that was already present. Mission meant inculturation and indigenisation. The age of spiritual colonisation had come to an end.

In the past thirty years the Church in the Philippines has been coming of age. Now almost all the bishops and most of the priests are native born. The religious life too is becoming indigenised. The laity are taking more and more responsibility. The missionaries' rôle is a supporting one rather than a leading one. They may not always like what they see happening but they must have trust and confidence. They must give way like a mother-in-law has to.

Christ also had to do this. He had to let go of his own home and his own mother. He prepared the field for others to plough and reap. These others were, humanly speaking, very weak and incompetent. The apostles were a cowardly gang. Peter was impulsive and unreliable, Thomas lacked faith, and Judas used to help himself from the common purse. Yet, he gave over the stage to them and they carried on the work in their own way.

Jesus trusted and accepted the very human instruments he had to work with as his Father had trusted him in his own weak humanity. We too must accept and trust and empower one another. If the missionary is to be true to Christ, he or she must give over and give way to the local Church in a Christ-like way.

But missionaries, like mothers-in-law, are sensitive people with big egos. They have to be able to hear those they have nurtured as they say, 'If you love us, you must let us do it our way,' or even, 'If you love us you must leave us altogether.' They have to be able to hear it with joy rather than resentment. The day they hear it, they day of their success, may humanly speaking be a very sad day. But if the missionary has been leaving self behind for twenty to thirty minutes each day in meditation, he or she will certainly find the grace to let go easily and enjoy the fullness of life that this detachment brings.

Being Evangelised by the Poor

I wished that I was not there! I was on the bus in the South of Mindanao going to visit the mother of Brother Joe. Joe and I had been together in community for fifteen years. On his Silver Jubilee of Profession he had been given a trip to Ireland. There it was discovered that he had cancer of the liver. His family had been informed but now I was bringing the news that it was only a matter of days until the end. I felt totally inadequate to console his family because, inside, I was in turmoil myself. I myself could not make any sense of what was happening and felt angry toward our so-called good God.

When I arrived at the nipa house, in the middle of the rice fields, his mother said in the Ilongo dialect, 'He's dead?' 'No,' I answered, 'but the news is not good.' She sniffled for a while and then, with all her quiet matriarchal dignity, said, 'Remember this, lad, whatever happens is a gift from heaven.' After a little while she said, 'He will be buried here?'

I explained how for many reasons it would be impossible to bring his body back to the Philippines. After another silence she said, 'When you don't see the body, the pain is doubled. But, remember this lad, whatever happens is a gift from heaven.'

I had gone to console and I was consoled. I had gone to bring faith but it was I who received it. I had gone to evangelise but it was she who evangelised me. This is one of the richest concepts that has emerged in the post Vatican II Church. Mission is not just to evangelise the poor (whatever kind of poverty it may be) but also to be evangelised in the process by the poor.

Let us take another example. One Sunday morning I took some visitors to a distant barrio. When I reached the chapel one of the local chapel leaders was conducting a service. He was one of those who came into the centre each month for training. He conducted the service admirably. Afterwards he spoke to my guests, 'What a pity,' he said, 'that we do not have a priest here to say Mass.' Something in my heart screamed, 'What a pity if we had a priest here!' What a pity that this man does not recognise the richness of the presence of Christ who is there where two or three are gathered in his name.

Yet another group was preparing for confession. They started by dividing up into groups and discussing the sinfulness in their neighbourhood. They discussed their own contribution to that sinfulness and what they could do to lessen it and atone for it. It was a beautiful ceremony of deep reconciliation. I stood by, listening to the process. I had been asked to administer the Sacrament of Reconciliation after this. I felt in my heart that it was the wrong thing to do. By my sacramental, almost magical act, the sacredness and power of what they had done was trivialised. Christ was probably more in their service of sharing than in my service of absolving.

I could go on and on giving examples of where people, by their words and acts, especially by their reflections on the word of God in times of stress, challenge our assumptions, our righteousness, and the structures which we assume are the only channels of God's presence.

The Second Vatican Council accepted the 'People of God' model of Church as the primary one. The Church, the people of God, is a sacrament or sign of the presence of God in the world. The Church is the people of God and so the people are the primordial sacrament. His presence is in people and they are his sacraments. For a long time we have been so emphasising the Real Presence in the Eucharist and the sacramental initiation in Baptism that our people fail to be aware of the equally real presence of God in people. We have tended to speak of the redemption as the first theological fact and Baptism as the only initiation into relationship with God, forgetting that God first created all things good and created human beings in his image and likeness. The Indian mystics say that God dances creation. The dancer is met in the dance. God is met in creation and speaks to us through it. God is in the wonderful discoveries and accomplishments of modern science and technology. But he is also in the words and actions of the poor. Our faith is challenged to recognise him and to be evangelised by him amongst them.

There is one clear example in the Gospel of how Christ himself was evangelised by the poor. In Matthew 15, Jesus is met by the Canaanite woman who asks him to have pity on her because her daughter is troubled by a demon. The woman is poor in many senses. In the culture of her day being a woman was to be poor and she was a foreign woman at that! She has no right to approach Jesus. She is poor also because of her daughter's plight.

When she approaches Jesus she puts him on the spot. By instinct he is a man of compassion but his self-understanding of his mission at this time is that he has been sent only to the lost sheep of Israel. He answers not a word; he pauses over his dilemma. He is pushed by the apostles to get rid of her and he tells her rather weakly what he understands his mission to be.

When she comes at him again he tells her, with the aggressiveness of the insecure, that it is not right to give the food of the children to dogs. She answers him back, 'Even the dogs eat the leavings that fall from the master's table.'

Her rejoinder is the last straw. 'Goodness gracious! ' he must have heard from within himself, 'This woman does have faith! These people can have faith. I am called to reach out to her and her kind.' His self understanding has been expanded by his encounter with this poor woman. He has been evangelised by her.

We see the extent to which he was evangelised a little while later in chapter twenty of the same gospel when he tells the story of the owner of the estate who went to employ labourers for his vineyard. Some he called at dawn, others at mid-morning and others at the eleventh hour. But all were paid the same. In this parable Jesus was saying that the late-comers, the non-Jews, would receive the same reward or place in his kingdom as the Jews themselves.

Now, what allowed Jesus to pause, what gave him the ability to reflect, the sensitivity to be affected by the woman on this occasion? I think it was the recurring theme, the background music, that we hear so frequently during the life of Jesus. 'He went apart to pray.' From his presence to his Father he gained a stillness, a poise, an alertness that enabled him to hear the Father's voice in the voices of the poor.

We too need to be open to being evangelised by the poor, to hearing the Lord speak through the poverties within us and around us, to question our assumptions, to soften our rigidities, to let go of our boxed-in concepts of how God should act. We will be able to do this only to the extent that we have stillness within ourselves, a stillness that can be cultivated by saying the Mantra for twenty to thirty minutes each morning and each evening.

Violence, Justice and Meditation

There is a Greek legend about an innkeeper called Procrustes. He was a rather odd fellow. He had this fixation about conformity. He wanted each of his guests to fit exactly into the allotted bed. 'Exactly' meant that if the guest was too tall he would have the head or feet hacked to shorten the person. He had a rack on hand to stretch those who needed lengthening.

This story is not altogether outlandish. There is an amazing tendency in all of us to be violent and to seek a quick short-term way of making others or the world accommodate to our personal view of how they or the world should be. Recently I heard of a nurse who was offered a scholarship to Canada. Her mother said to her, 'You know that I have high blood pressure. If you go I may have a stroke and you will be responsible.' This puts the daughter in a terrible dilemma: if she went she would be anxious and guilty; if she stayed she would be angry and frustrated at the way her mother had manipulated her. The relationship between mother and daughter is shattered by the violence of the no-win option the mother has set upon her child.

Violence is a frequent reality in our homes. If it is not physical violence it is psychological violence. A girl gets pregnant. The short-term solution is a violent one, an abortion. Subtle forms of violence exist wherever people live together. People can use their 'feelings' as a way of blocking discussion or change in a community. Being late, being slow, or getting sick may sometimes be forms of passive-agressive behaviour, and in their own way, manifest violence.

In the political field we see the same impatience and seeking of violent short-term solutions. Many right wing governments, particularly in Third World countries, condone the extra-juridical elimination of those perceived to be threats to national security. There is considerable evidence that such action is approved by the governments of First World countries. Similarly, terrorists and national liberation armies use violence to achieve their objectives.

Frightful injustice is a reality of our world and indeed very often, of family life. It needs great energy, indeed passion, to confront and fight injustice. To be a true Christian we are often called to 'be angry but do not sin.' (Eph 4:26) Christ himself was justifiably angry when he saw his house desecrated. Christ's house may either be a temple of stone or living human beings, the temples of the poor on whom the Pharisees laid unbearable burdens.

It is only when we have experienced injustice ourselves – and we all have in some way – that we can empathise with those who suffer and be in solidarity with their cause. I remember a priest telling me that whenever he sees a person in a big car – especially a bishop – he gets angry. He remembers how, when he was a little boy, the landlord came in a big car and ordered their house burned down. This memory gives him a great feeling for the oppressed and dispossessed. This feeling is a grace but it is a grace only if it is Christianised. To be active and constructive, that anger must be tamed. Our own experience of being treated unjustly gives us sensitivity to the injustices suffered by others. This is a source of energy. But if we have not come to terms with our own anger, we will be fighting a supposed monster outside without realising that the real one is inside. The great danger of fighting monsters is that we can easily become monsters ourselves in the process.

Justice is often another word for vengeance, misplaced vengeance, directed towards authority or authority figures. The Russian writer Solzynitzen says, 'The line between good and bad, between just and unjust, between oppressor and oppressed, does not pass between nations, or groups within nations. It passes first through the human heart.' Unless we can deal with it first in our hearts we will only be countersigns in preaching the gospel of justice.

The great problem about justice then is spirituality, just as the great problem about spirituality is justice. Fighting for justice without a deep spirituality is as great a tragedy as those who claim to be spiritual and are not concerned about justice. Fighting for justice without spirituality has often led to burn-out, loss of religious vocation, and to the taking up of arms.

To be committed to justice we must first have heard our own pain at its depth. We must have learned to sit with our anger and to befriend our negative feelings. If not, these feelings will clutter up the doors of our hearts and minds, and make rational, just and consistent action impossible. We must learn to be patient, to wait. It does not help anyone if we compound the present violence with our own kind of violence.

Meditation, I believe, is the best preparation for work for justice. I might say that one who does not have a deep contemplative life is a liability in this work. He or she should be wearing a T-Shirt bearing the words, 'I am a dangerous person.'

In the process of meditation one hears the totality of oneself. One goes down through the layers of anger and hatred to the sense of justice and peace that is at the heart of Christ. One learns the practice and balance of Christ himself.

While Christ preached justice passionately, it was not his priority value – mercy and compassion were. We too cannot preach justice if our hearts are not filled with compassion and mercy.

Where can we realistically begin to change the world except in ourselves? We must first align our passions and bring them to bear on the problems constructively. This may lead one to research, another to legal aid, another to organising amongst the poor. Ultimately it leads to a reverence not only for the sufferers but also for those who have been dehumanised into causing the suffering. It leads to the poverty of realising that only the oppressed themselves can liberate the oppressed and that all that an outsider can do is to be in solidarity with them.

Meditation gives one the only weapon a disciple can have to deal with bullies. I have seen a number of times how people of violence cannot deal with the presence of a contemplative. We need contemplative presence, not armies, to stand up against violence. The figures of Dom Helder Camera and Archbishop Romero come quickly to mind in this context. I also see Fr Bernard Häring, who in his old age can make this kind of stance for the right of conscience, even against the power of the Vatican. His power is in his contemplative calm. It is the only power that we need and can use in the face of injustice and violence. A key way to this power is the twice daily saying of the Mantra.

Mary: Contemplation and Action

The angel said to Mary, 'Even your relative Elizabeth is expecting a son in her old age, although she was unable to have a child, and she is now in her sixth month. With God nothing is impossible.' Then Mary said, 'I am the servant of the Lord, let it be done to me as you have said.' And the angel left her.

Mary set out for a town in the hills of Judah. She entered the house of Zachariah and greeted Elizabeth... Mary remained with Elizabeth for about three months and then returned home. (Luke 1:36-40, 56)

When we read the gospel passages about Our Lady we notice two things in particular: her contemplative nature and her loving activity. We find her listening to God as he speaks to her through the angel who tells her that she is to be the mother of Christ. We find her pondering the shepherds' words and the words of her son in the temple, pondering them in her heart. Her prayerful heart, and the tradition it gave rise to, gave forth the *Magnificat*.

Meditation is deep listening. Listening to the Mantra in silence trains one to listen for God wherever he is in life. It then calls the heart to compassionate response.

We all know that love is the greatest of the commandments and that it is shown in love for our neighbour. However, when it comes to concrete situations this command to love becomes very difficult. If you give locally you become known as a soft touch and then you are inundated with sob stories. You may become a Santa Claus to whom everybody runs for help, or an oak tree under whose great shadow other sprouts cannot grow. You can contribute generously to a Third World country and then one day you read in the newspapers about the percentage that goes into administration, or of rip offs, or of corruption in the country being helped, or even of the adverse effects your aid may be having on the people that you want to help.

It takes a lot of listening to the situation to give wisely. The contemplative Mary seemed to have that gift. She could distinguish when it was appropriate to give, or to just put in a good word, or to provide psychological support.

At the Annunciation she was informed that Elizabeth was to have a child. As a woman she knew that her cousin would need another woman around the house. She got on her donkey and headed for Ain Karem. Action was needed and she took it.

Again at Cana of Galilee, she was tuned in to the situation. She saw that the wine was running out so she put in a good word with Jesus, 'They have no wine.' There was no demanding or imploring – just a confident statement of need.

On many other occasions we find her in a supportive rôle. She was often in the background when Jesus preached. She was at the foot of the cross. She was with the terrified disciples in the upper room after the death of Jesus.

So too with us in our ministry, sometimes we give, financially or by doing things for people. Sometimes a word is just the right thing, words can give life and sometimes too they can bring death – even well-intentioned words. Most often our greatest effectiveness is in the things that we support and empower others to do.

Like Mary, we all need comtemplative wisdom to distinguish one kind of helping from the other and to choose the appropriate one. That is why the twice daily meditation is very important for one who wants to love wisely, as Mary did.